SOULFIRE WOMAN

How To Torch Your Past, Ignite Your Present And Set Your Soul On Fire

DYANNE KELLEY, M.S.

Copyright © 2019 by Dyanne Kelley

All rights reserved. No part of this publication may be reproduced, distributed or transmitted in any form or by any means, including photocopying, recording, or other electronic or mechanical methods, without the prior written permission of the publisher, except in the case of brief quotations embodied in critical reviews and certain other noncommercial uses permitted by copyright law. For permission requests, write to the publisher, at the address below.

Quantity sales: Special discounts are available on quantity purchases by nonprofit organizations, corporations, associations, clubs and others.
For details, contact us at PositivelyPoweredPublications.com

Positively Powered Publications
Louisville, CO
PositivelyPoweredPublications.com

Cover Design: Melody Christian of FinickyDesigns.com
Project Editor: Amy Collette
Proofreading Editor: Alexandra O'Connell

SOULFIRE WOMAN / Dyanne Kelley—1st ed.

Library of Congress Control Number: 2019909878

ISBN: 978-1-7329022-7-5

Disclaimer: Although every effort has been made to provide the best possible information in this book, neither the publisher nor author is responsible for accidents, injuries or damage incurred as a result of use or misuse of this information. This book is not a substitute for professional services.

Praise for
Soulfire Woman

"A joy to read. I want to buy this book for every woman I know. Part how-to book, part workbook, part memoir, *Soulfire Woman* speaks to Every Woman. Reminiscent at times of Elizabeth Gilbert's journey to find her true self, Kelley writes with grace, humor, empathy and faith. She believes that every woman can find the 'Soulfire Woman' she's meant to be. At a time when too many writers are telling us there's magic in not giving a f*ck or that we need to be badasses, Kelley's journey and truths are profound and inspiring. The activities provided help you find the you who's always been there. There is so much truth in this book, things we might've known as girls and forgotten, that it evokes a sense of nostalgia and hope for the future. It's packed with practical advice on how to achieve a soulful life, how to thrive and not just survive. I am a Soulfire Woman in progress. I highly recommend this book."

—Michele Young-Stone, author of *Lost in the Beehive*

"In league with so many of the luminaries mentioned in the resource section of her book, Dyanne Kelley can proudly add *Soulfire Woman* to this list. With adroit clarity, Dyanne has paved a path of practical application of oftentimes seemingly out-of-reach spiritual principles. Whether it's in your own journal or via a circle of women, using Ms. Kelley's invitations will assuredly lead you to your truest, most powerful and empowered Self. In these times of copious spiritual ideology, Soulfire Woman provides an authentic, intimate engagement at the level of your soul. So much so, in fact, I'll be adding this to our Modern Day Priestess Training recommended reading list. Thank you for your undaunting Yes, Dyanne!"

—Rev. Dr. Kate Rodger, founder,
Institute of Modern Wisdom

"Soulfire Woman inspires us to take a powerful journey with the author, moving us away from the pain of past experiences. This book is a wonderful map to becoming the heroine of our own stories, and also to live within sacredness and divinity."

—Karen Bachman

"Loved this book, it felt like coming home. It speaks to your inner spirit, and it felt so right to me that I felt as if I was meditating inside a circle of trust and love as I was reading it. Dyanne shares her personal experiences to keep this very real and to remind us that we all are amazing and worthy."

—Jill Yocum

"A true gem for women of all ages! While the more seasoned of us might naturally feel a connection to the Simone de Beauvoir-esque psyche of the protagonist, this book offers great lessons in living for Soulfire Women younger and older alike. As such you are likely to come back and read it time and again and to want to gift it to other women in your life."
—Andréa Cantarelli, Ph.D.

"Discover true freedom. Learn to listen to your body, feelings and true self through the exercises and teachings throughout the book. Be honest with yourself. Do the work and you will embrace your inner Soulfire Woman."
—Cindy

"Dyanne's brave journey is her own, yet in it we can find our own path of self discovery and healing. Follow Dyanne's seven paths; take what you need, use what you can. I loved the Soulfire Woman Principles. Remember, 'Lasting change is created from within. We all have a higher purpose.' This gem of a book can help you find yours."
—MCL

"The author shares some challenging life situations, and her search for various modalities that help her grow and move forward in life physically, mentally, and spiritually. If her life were a labyrinth, she has reached the center and become 'a woman who is one unto herself.' Now on her path, like the departing from the labyrinth, she is writing to guide; supporting, holding other women on their personal journeys. I will need to read this several times to absorb all the richness."

—PJ Teal

Bonus Material

Let's walk the
Soulfire Woman's Way together.
Visit http://soulfirewoman.com/bonus
for exclusive access to my guided
meditations, video recordings and
more, just for readers of
Soulfire Woman.

Dedication

Dedicated to you, Soulfire Woman, for your courage to heal, reclaim who you really are, and step into your power.

"You are not your story. You are what you do with your story. And so much more." ~Dyanne Kelley

Table of Contents

Introduction i
PART I: TORCHING THE PAST 1
   Reclaim Your Power: A Primal Call to Authenticity 3
   Know What You Know 25
PART II: IGNITING YOUR PRESENT 45
   Feel To Heal..47
   Get Into Your Body: Connecting Mind, Body and
   Soulfire..61
PART III: SETTING YOUR SOUL ON FIRE 73
   Open Your Heart...75
   Freedom: Stepping Into Soulfire Woman Power 89
   Live a Higher-Consciousness Life On Purpose.............101

   Book Club Questions 111
   Resources 113
   In Gratitude..119
   About Dyanne..121

Introduction

SOULFIRE WOMAN: HOW TO TORCH YOUR PAST, IGNITE YOUR PRESENT AND SET YOUR SOUL ON FIRE is the true Heroine's Journey. It's my story. It's your story. It's a woman's story, an inner journey of healing and wisdom and a reclaiming of our authentic Divine Feminine Soulfire. Every woman I have worked with as a psychotherapist and healer is somewhere on this journey. After witnessing and working with so many women trying to literally find themselves amidst their given and assumed roles in life, through their duties and obligations, and once found, trying to create a sense of self-worth and purpose, I saw that there is a distinct pathway, a yellow brick road to our inner selves. The Soulfire Woman's Way awakens us to healing and finding our way back to authenticity and wholeness, to meaning and purpose, to our Divine Feminine Power—a pathway unique to women. It begins with a burning desire, a fire in the Soul to live life fully, to feel alive and be who we are meant to be. Once that desire is ignited there is no turning back.

You will recognize yourself in the story, I'm sure. The one thing that unites women is our stories. These stories are the very platforms needed for healing and growing and finding our way home. Too often, though, we get stuck in the story; we stay in the pretty little box and fail to claim our most powerful selves. The Heroine's Journey is the one where life is going along fine, you are performing your many roles and duties nicely, until one day the floor drops beneath you, plunging you into the depths of awakening, finding your true self beyond the roles you play. This is also a naturally occurring process at midlife, the search for the woman you lost along the way or in answer to the question, "What's next?" Every woman finds herself at some point on this journey. I am also witnessing more and more women choosing self-discovery and healing at a younger age.

You overcome the barriers, heal yourself from past hurts and traumas, strip away layer by layer what you thought you knew to be true and drop the facades of your previous existence. Vulnerable and exposed, you have no choice but to surrender to what is your current reality and trust in a consciousness beyond your ego and physical self. (Well, you do have the choice to continue as is. Do you really want that?)

You are at the beginning, an authentic inner journey of rediscovery. Who am I really? Who do I want to be? What is my purpose?

In this rediscovery and healing path you learn to love and forgive the hardest-to-forgive person of all, yourself. You reach out to all the women who have gone before you who circle and embrace you with love, kindness and understanding; Soulfire women at work. You emerge, rise up from the depths full of hard-earned wisdom knowing exactly who you are (the answers were within all along, my dear), put on your ruby slippers and step into your Soulfire Feminine Power. *You* are the heroine of your own story.

Divine Feminine Power is the power of relationships, wisdom, unity, harmony, love, compassion, creativity, beauty, strength (physical and emotional), sexuality, and courage. We women need each other, the world needs us, to be our most powerful selves, to be healed, to know our own strength and use it for the good of all living beings ... to step into our most sacred powerful selves!

I used my own story to demonstrate the Soulfire Woman's Way to awakening and divided it into three parts: Torching Your Past; Igniting Your Present; and Setting Your Soul on Fire. This journey follows a pathway—your yellow brick road—where you will find markers essential to a woman's way of knowing and healing. They are: Reclaim Your Power; Know What You Know; Feel to Heal; Get Into Your Body; Open Your Heart; Freedom; and Live a Higher Consciousness Life on Purpose. Within each of these are specific tasks for women who truly want to heal and live an authentic and fulfilling life. At the end of each chapter, you'll find Soulfire Woman Principles (what's true for women), Spiritual Lessons (what's true for everyone), and Psychological Truths (what you need to know to heal), followed by Torching Your Past, Igniting Your Present, and Setting Your Soul on Fire action steps, the how-to of healing and moving forward.

You can work through the book any number of ways. You may want to read the whole story first and then go back and "do the work." You may want to take one chapter at a time and stay with it until you feel complete before you move on to the next. Or, you may want to work through it all simultaneously, picking and choosing what you need most. There actually is no real order or sequence; however, the tasks within each chapter are essential to create a Soulfire Woman life.

You may also decide you don't want to do it alone and choose to have individual Soulfire Woman sessions to help you along the way and keep you focused. Any way you choose is fine. There are no rules! This is important for women; no rules, only *choices*. You will intuitively know the right path.

Thank you so much for taking this journey with me. I am honored and humbled, and wish you the best in the rediscovery of your unique, beautiful, most magnificent self!

PART I:
TORCHING THE PAST

Reclaim Your Power: A Primal Call to Authenticity

Choosing yourself is one of the greatest acts of self-love and compassion available to you. It alone shifts the balance of power within you.

Moment of Reckoning

I'VE DEDICATED MY LIFE TO HEALING myself and others. At first out of necessity to save myself, and then to share with others how to heal and live a truly authentic life. As a psychotherapist, I've worked with thousands of women and witnessed with honor and humility what helps others heal. I call myself a keeper of stories. I hold stories too painful for women to hold themselves and keep them, the women and their stories, in a womb-like container, warm, nurturing, safe and secure. I hold them there until they are ready for rebirth, to come into the light, breathing new life—whoosh—with startling revelations and awakenings. My psychotherapy training was traditional, although I knew it was divinely guided from the start. When I look back over the years now, I can see just how divinely guided life really is. There are some who believe we choose our lifetimes before we say yes to being. Well, if I did, I chose one heck of a ride!

I share my own story not because the story is important. It really isn't. What is important is that I am no longer my story. What is important is what I did with my story. It's not about blame or who did what to me or hard feelings. It's about transformation and how my story helped me find my way back to who I am. I tell it so you know I am you. And you are me. We all have a story. I could start almost anywhere. My story of emotional and physical healing is not linear. It loops, goes sideways, backwards and forwards; it spirals. There is no real beginning. And as for the end, well, insight and healing are like a woven tapestry—the edges expand with each new row, creating a richer, more beautiful, more colorful cloth.

Where I will start is the very moment I recognized, like a lightning bolt from heaven, that the whole premise on which I based my identity was a sham, false, not really me. It was carefully designed and orchestrated over my childhood and young adulthood to be liked, to be loved, to hide my imperfections, and most importantly not to be abandoned. I would go to any lengths not to be abandoned. Yet that's exactly what happened. And it was a blessing.

By outward appearances I looked successful. I was married to a handsome, intelligent husband, had a great job and a young daughter. I was doing it all, a young working mom with a demanding executive position, and a wife with a home. Yet I felt guilty all the time. When my daughter was sick, I felt guilty not being at home with her if I chose to go to work, and guilty if I chose to stay home and miss work.

The story line then was that women could do it all, and there was something wrong with you if you didn't manage with aplomb. The feminist movement was in full swing, and as women we were fighting desperately to get out of the house—a good thing—and add to our personal fulfillment through meaningful work. We truly believed we could do it all without consequence. All I managed to do was feel exhausted and guilty. There was no Amazon Prime saving me time by delivering much-needed items to my doorstep. No meals arrived in a box with all the necessary ingredients to cook our dinner; the closest grocery store was ten miles away. If I didn't have milk or eggs for a recipe, I ran to the neighbor's house across the street. The internet hadn't arrived yet for quick instructions on how to fix the running toilet or to come up with something quick to eat. And, there were no daycare facilities. The county ran a program where children were placed in private homes. Pick-up time was strict: 5:30 p.m. We had an hour commute time, which caused added daily pressure. Three late strikes and you lost your daycare spot. When I picked up my daughter at daycare, the table was always set with the delicious aroma of dinner greeting me at the door, a reminder to be prompt and of how hungry I was. Did I even know what we were having for dinner?

Something wasn't right at home either. My husband was distant, communicated little and acted unhappy. He repeatedly insisted nothing was wrong. I believed his words, not his actions. I hadn't learned yet how to trust my gut and my intuition, and to trust actions over words. I certainly wanted to believe him. I don't remember quite how I found out, by accident I'm sure, except *there are no accidents*. I realized in one stunning moment that my husband was having an affair with a much younger female co-worker.

Really? How could this happen? Like I said, it was a different time. Women did it all without complaint. There was no sharing in the diaper changing or housework. Or maybe I just didn't ask. Or maybe I just got tired of asking. My husband worked. I worked *and* carried the balance of the household duties. I strove to be deliberately perfect in every way. That was how I felt loved of course, by what I did for others. I worked. I cooked. I cleaned. I made myself beautiful. I starved myself to be thin, losing my baby weight as fast as I could. I exercised. I asked very little of him. I gave all of my power away. I gave it to him to decide if I was thin enough, pretty enough, and whatever enough. How could he possibly want anyone or anything else?

What was not good enough? Not good enough is a theme that would repeat itself over and over again. I often wonder, do men ever feel not good enough or is this an affliction of women?

It's very hard to explain those moments of realization when it all makes sense. I had the revelation that if all I had done to be perfect did not manifest how I believed it would, having a perfect home, family, loving husband, successful career, being a great mom, then where did it leave me? I knew I no longer had to do all the things I was doing to keep my husband, my image and my job because it didn't work. I lost my husband (I thought) and disliked my job in public relations, which was based on outward appearances and distorting the truth to fit an image. Life imitating life. If none of these things worked to attain my goals, then I no longer had to do them, right? I actually remember feeling tremendous relief in the moment. I could do what I wanted. All along I had done what everyone else wanted, and it didn't matter one iota. Not one iota. Being someone else for someone else or for an organization does not work.

As far as I could tell, I could keep going as I was, being clearly untrue to myself, or I could try to figure out who I was, or who I wanted to be. Reality struck again. After all those years of losing myself in others I had no idea of who I was.

It felt scary, like fear-of-drowning scary, this not knowing at all who I was. What if I was nobody? What if I didn't like the real me? What if no one liked me? I knew for sure I had sold my soul in exchange for a sense of security, both in work and relationships. I wasn't connected to my feelings. I submerged them, pretended they didn't exist for fear a big reveal would cause me to lose the people closest to me—my family, friends and co-workers. I was afraid I couldn't handle my own true feelings. I had the reputation of being someone who never got angry. So I smiled and really thought I was happy all the time. I really did. I believed the story I told myself. Sadness, anger, disappointment? Nope, not in my vocabulary. I could withstand anything. I was tough, a survivor of a more-than-challenging childhood (which is where the abandonment thing comes in). Nothing was going to bring me down. Not now. Not ever.

Until it did.

Sounding like you yet?

I would like to say here that I picked myself up by my bootstraps with this new realization and went off with my independent feminist attitude to find myself and save the world. Nope. Didn't do that. My unconscious fears of abandonment, not feeling good enough, and being unlovable were much stronger and deeper than my realization of the truth of who I was or wasn't and what I needed to do to be true to myself. I could still fake it. I don't think I knew then that these feelings were tethering and containing me, keeping me tied in a marriage where I was not appreciated or respected, trapped in my fears. Fear of not knowing myself, and maybe not even liking myself, was too much for me to absorb. Not having the person I was married to be in love with me was more than I could bear. It wounded me to my very core. Why wasn't I lovable? What was wrong with me? I could only handle a glimpse of that truth before the shutter would close again, a quick snapshot of reality. I most definitely did not want to be alone with myself and all that I thought I needed to fix.

I knew in my heart I wasn't strong enough emotionally to be on my own right then. I didn't know where I would go or what I would do on my own with a 2-year-old and a career I came to realize was not me at all. I was afraid. I fell into the abyss, a dark hole of sadness, of nothingness. All those feelings I never knew I had collapsed into one big one: depression. "Anger turned inward," some like to say. I cried. I begged. I emotionally manipulated to keep my marriage together, believing this was the only thing I knew for sure. I thought I knew my husband better than he knew himself and that he was making a big mistake. I was what was best for him. After all, I supported him emotionally and helped him move along in his career. In my mind, I did everything. That's what I did in order to be loved. Everything.

Meanwhile I barely told a soul. Only my soul knew the truth. I knew on some level that I was compromising my soul out of fear. Fear of my own empty shell. Fear of the unknown. Fear of change. Fear of being on my own. Fear of all that I needed to face deep within myself. Fear of what I would find. I had no identity if I wasn't attached to him. It was much easier pretending to be someone else, right?

We reconciled and began again, much to my relief. We started counseling—my husband agreed to two sessions. I continued on my own. He started his own business, whose first six-month contract took him to New England. I was in rural Pennsylvania, on my own with a toddler in an old house. The kitchen flooded the first week he was gone. We got snowed in time and time again that winter. When his contract got renewed for another six months with more possible extensions after that, I thought, "That's it. I'm willing to give up my position to be a normal family. How can we work on a marriage if we are apart more than we are together?" I was hell-bent on saving my marriage and family. I quit my good-paying job with benefits and security to follow him. Besides, I had always been drawn to New England. Why should he be alone living by the beautiful sea without me? It was going to be great.

I packed up the car and off I went, toddler in tow. I was barely in the door when the phone started ringing. Wrong number. Again. Wrong number. Again. Wait a minute, what? I stopped answering. I stood still and scanned the room. A dark blue folder stuck out of the top of a small garbage can. I took the folder and looked inside. Plane tickets with the other woman's name on them stared back at me.

Realization hovered in suspended animation, descending, descending, then igniting every fiber of my being now combustible. I moved out-of-body, watching myself in slow motion as I understood just what was happening. I went ballistic. Really ballistic. All those years of pent-up anger raging and spewing out of me. I was barely recognizable, even to myself—especially to myself. I think I shocked him for the first time. Maybe I wasn't the one who never got angry. I took a stand. I called my parents, who drove all the way from Pennsylvania and drove us back home that same day. I walked out.

I filed for divorce. My lawyer told me the best thing for our daughter was to share custody with my husband, switching back and forth every few days. I knew in my heart and soul this was not good for her. There would be no routine, no sense of security. I felt my resolve weakening. Could I really do this?

When I thought it couldn't get any worse, my daughter was hospitalized and quarantined until doctors figured out she had orbital cellulitis, an infection behind the eye. She started with a cold and then had a red bump under her eye I thought initially was a mosquito bite until the swelling got worse. I was lectured by the doctor. "Mother, you should have gotten her in sooner!" Yet another layer of guilt. She was kept in what looked like a cage, with me sleeping in a sleeper chair day and night beside her. She needed intravenous antibiotics and a port put in her hand. I wasn't allowed to take her out and hold her. She would stand in there and cry. I would cry. Of course, I would reach in and get her, rock and soothe her until one of the nurses found me and told me to put her back. They were afraid of the chair getting infected. Seriously, that's the truth. It couldn't be disinfected.

This was a time before cell phones. I had no idea where my husband was. My resolve weakened even more. I was at my breaking point.

My husband said it wasn't how it looked, that he was ending the affair, not resuming it. It was the last encounter, he said. OK, now I had no job. Living with my parents was not going to work in the long run, there was too much baggage and unfinished business. My husband wanted to stay together, or so he said. I wanted and I needed to believe him. The balance of power had shifted in my direction, I thought. This was what I needed to buy some time and pull myself together emotionally.

I agreed to reconcile, with a plan to delay getting divorced until I felt stable and capable of following through with it. I decided I could not realistically move forward until I was emotionally stronger. I would work on finding a new career that made sense to me. I was no longer doing it for him, I was doing it for me. I chose myself for the first time in my life.

Choosing yourself is one of the greatest acts of self-love and compassion available to you. It alone shifts the balance of power within you. You learn not to be dependent on external sources for validation of your very existence. This knowledge would strengthen with time. I would take whatever time I needed to recover and build strength. I would get to know my daughter. I felt she spent way too many hours with her caregivers to the point that she had their accent, not ours. I needed to reclaim her, to be her mother. Only then would I reassess my situation and figure out what came next.

Then I did the unthinkable. I allowed myself to feel. The bottom dropped out. All I could feel was the black tar of sadness oozing over me, holding me in place, unable to move. How do I heal from this? How do I survive, again, emotional pain heaping onto past pain, piling higher and higher? I'm gulping, sinking beneath the surface, swallowing water.

I did not let on how I felt, except to my closest friends and family. I was much too guarded (and still perfect) for that. I pretended to be happy and smiling—my well-honed survival techniques. And, of course, all of our new friends thought we were the perfect couple. I knew the truth, though. Awareness had found me and wasn't leaving. I knew

Dyanne Kelley

I had no identity, that I was lost in the dark depths of the ocean trying to swim to the surface. Without a self, how could I survive? I knew I was dependent on many things, on a man who thought of his gratification first at my expense, on a false identity, on a Barbie doll image in a make-believe happy life. I knew I was dependent because I wasn't strong enough to stand on my own.

And this is what I did. I accepted it. I accepted that I wasn't perfect. Seeing clearly that I wasn't perfect may sound like it was easy. It wasn't. It meant I had to give up the one tool that made me feel presentable to the outside world. I stood face-to-face with reality and accepted the truth of imperfect me in that moment. I wasn't superwoman. I wasn't emotionally strong. This is where my transformation began: right here at this very moment of acceptance. I accepted all of my newfound realizations and awareness and that I wasn't ready to make a change yet. It was too scary. I didn't beat myself up. It was my own, silent personal truth.

Silent truth, the truth only you in your heart and the Divine know, creates a powerful internal shift like plate tectonics pushing against each other. It redefines your internal landscape. Your own truth will always create movement in the direction of your authentic self. I vowed to myself that I was going to get stronger, I would figure it out and become emotionally independent. I just didn't know how. By "accepted" I don't mean I felt resigned. I mean I accepted what was real about me and my situation. I didn't escape to Pretendville. Acceptance is like a reality check. It's also an action word. Once you accept your truth, an action step follows.

The fake me wasn't working for me anymore. Maybe she never did. Now I was finally ready to admit it, if only to myself. Truth is not always pretty. Pretty had left the building. Wisdom and growth started making their way through the open door. I could feel the flame of my Soulfire lighting. With that small spark I began to see the path of the Soulfire Woman's Way.

Committing to the One Person Who Matters Most, You

This was my moment of reckoning. A moment in time when I realized what I was doing was not getting me the results I wanted, when I knew in the depths of my soul that I needed to change for my own survival.

It's about survival of the self. It's when you deliberately, unequivocally, and with intent choose you over anyone else. You, at your core, your essence, must survive. Your Soulfire begins to burn. There is no other decision to make. It is your birthright. You say yes to the only person you have any control over, yourself.

Here is where you start: by opening the door to honesty. Accepting truth, what is real, with raw, gut-wrenching honesty only you need to know, is the way home to yourself. Accepting without judgment, no self-criticisms. Accepting your reality with the compassion of a friend telling you her story, knowing that you did not end up this way overnight. All those false parts of yourself, how you evolved, how you behaved and presented yourself to the world, you did for your own reasons—to cope mainly; to survive. These coping methods usually work for a while, even a good portion of your life. Eventually they stop working because they are based on a false identity, your inauthentic self. The moment of reckoning is when you stop pretending. No more illusions.

If you want your life to change—if you want to find your way back home to who you are—you have to get down and dirty with yourself, get real. And it's all OK. It was OK for me to admit I wasn't ready to change everything in an instant. Awareness is change. Awareness is the beginning of wisdom and transformation. Once your eyes are open to the truth you will automatically propel yourself in the right direction even if you stand still for a while. Time is irrelevant here. It will take however long it takes. There have been many times in my life where I needed to be hit with a spiritual two-by-four to move forward. Yup, clunked on the head. It doesn't matter where or when you get on the path. Just get on it.

Choose You.

Soulfire Woman Principles

You are a Soulfire Woman. You have within you an untouched part of yourself, your core, your essence, the keeper of the truth of who you are, your original source of light, your flame. It's the part of you, a pure higher self that connects you to the greater Universe. When you open this portal, all things are possible.

Choose You. Your well-being comes before all else. There is nothing else without this. Choose SoulFULL instead of SelfLESS. SelfLESS gets no respect, not even from yourself—especially not from yourself. SelfLESS is exactly how you lose your power. Step into your full expression of yourself. Step into your full power.

Your power is important. Do not give your power away. It's emotionally and energetically deflating. Every time you swallow your truth, you're giving your power away. When you let things happen, instead of making a choice, you're giving your power away. Soulfire Women are equal parts warriors, lovers, Earth Mothers and creators, priestesses and wisdom keepers. Remember that. Every Soulfire Woman has a warrior within her.

You already are perfection. You were born perfect. Perfection is who you uniquely are even before you enter the world, encoded with your genes, abilities and desires. You do not need external validation to be perfect. Perfection does not require striving, especially striving to be somebody else. It just is. It is within you. You are it. Let it shine through like sunshine bursting through your core. Remember who you are.

Compassion starts with you for you. Compassion does not mean feel sorry for yourself, although I believe there is an important place for this. Compassion is an active word. It means love and action. Loving Action directed straight at your own heart.

Trust your gut. Trust your gut. Trust your gut. Remember, my dear, you had the answers within all along.

Spiritual Lessons

Allow yourself to see and receive. Give yourself permission to see what is both in front of you and within you. Don't worry. Your psyche, precious thing, will only allow you to see what you need to see at any given moment. It's like driving a car at night with the headlights on. You can only see so many feet in front of you. Trust in your highest self to know what's best for you. Receive it with an open heart.

Once you allow yourself to really see, you are on the road to becoming aware. Now you know the truth. Deep-in-your-bones truth. When you are aware, there's no turning back. You can choose to do nothing, and this is a perfectly acceptable choice, but you cannot become unaware. Truth-telling sets you free. Have faith in this.

Accept your reality in the moment. Denying and pretending something isn't true expends a lot of unnecessary energy. It also blocks your psychological, spiritual and physical energy. This is how you get sick. Your body becomes the container for your untruths and secrets, holds them for you, and creates dis-ease around them. Once you accept your reality, you physically and energetically release and are able to make clearer decisions. The Universe begins its co-creation with you, putting your intentions and prayers into motion.

If you do these things, your body, mind and soul will begin to connect the dots. The dots create a pathway, your yellow brick road, the Soulfire Woman Way. You will begin to propel yourself consciously and unconsciously toward wholeness.

There are no accidents. One way of thinking about this is, we as humans make meaning and purpose out of what happens to us as a way of surviving, thriving and growing in Spirit. Another way is that the Universe works on your behalf to bring your conscious and unconscious desires into existence seemingly like magic. Bumping into the right person at just the right time is synchronicity, a meaningful coincidence. When you are in the midst of transformation, synchronicities appear like flowers in springtime.

Psychological Truths

Sometimes you have to go backwards before you can move forward. If your unconscious past is making decisions for you in the present, then you have to clear the past. By unconscious I mean you are unaware of your psychological wounds and patterns. When you make your unconscious conscious, it opens the channels for awareness, which opens up the channels for transformation. You need to become aware psychologically, spiritually, physically and energetically. You know your unconscious past is making decisions for you when you have behaviors you cannot seem to change or feelings like shame or unworthiness that are ever present. Depression and anxiety often come from unresolved issues. These issues can be in your lifetime, can be genetically encoded and passed down to you, and some believe can come from other lifetimes. For example, I have an irrational fear of being poor and destitute and was told by an energy healer I was shunned from my tribe in a past life and left to fend for myself. It could further explain why the fear of abandonment rises to the surface in my current life.

Everyone has a core issue ... or two. This is usually a deep-seated fear of some sort. Fear of rejection, fear of abandonment, fear of being unlovable, fear of unworthiness.... These create patterns of behavior and contribute to unconscious choices. If unhealthy patterns keep repeating themselves, then chances are you haven't found and resolved your core issue(s). As you follow the

Soulfire Woman's Way, these issues will come into the light, be tossed into the fire, and burned off as you work the principles and move along the path.

You are not your story. You are what you do with your story. And so much more.

Torching Your Past

Everything in life is energy, which is never lost or destroyed. It just changes its element. When you torch something, you clear it like a controlled burn in a forest. It is then free for new growth; a phoenix rising from the ashes. It is transformed. Transformation is life-giving and exciting. Think of it as an upgrade from surviving to thriving; a new way of living, being, thinking and behaving. Your inner space is cleared, igniting and illuminating your present; life as it really is right now. You will be able to live in the moment and not the past. Tuning in to the present opens up a whole new world of possibilities—you find your authentic self amid the ashes. It's intoxicating becoming who you were always meant to be. Your soul sets on fire. Remember this as you shine a light on some of the more difficult parts of your story. If you feel like you might need support as you work your way through the Soulfire Woman's Way, go to soulfirewoman.com to find additional resources. If you feel like your world is rocked, and you are on emotionally shaky ground, I highly recommend finding a psychotherapist who can support you.

Your moment of reckoning. Is it here? Have you reached the point where you know you can't continue as you are without losing more of yourself? When what you are doing in life is driving holes into your soul, deflating you at every turn? Declare this as your moment of reckoning. Declare it in every possible way—shout it, stomp it, be it. Say it with determination. It all stops and starts here, the end of life as you know it and the beginning of your new authentic life. Tell yourself you are worth saving, how much you deserve this, and how brave you are.

Make a commitment. Look in the mirror and make a commitment to yourself, your soul, your innermost being, your highest, wisest self. What are you saying yes to? What is it you are committing to exactly? Why? Be specific. This will determine your path. What do you want your new, authentic life to look like? How do you want it to feel? Write and rewrite it until it feels right, deep down in your bones. Write it in the present tense like it is already happening. Write it as a declaration and sign it.

Draw it. Collage it. Dance it. Post it in view. Look at it every day.

Be kind to yourself. Create a long list of things that nurture you and bring you joy. Then do them. Get really good at doing them. The road ahead may not be easy. It's going to be like dolphin diving. You can go deep for periods of time, and then you come up for air. It helps to be able to retreat and renew as often as possible.

Make another list of things that ground you: walking barefoot in the grass or sand, nature, gardening, cooking, art-making, baths, deep breathing, gathering crystals like black tourmaline, star gazing, sun and moon bathing, yoga. Yoga is like a personal container; it brings awareness to your breath and body, focuses your mind and builds inner and outer strength. Yoga represents life. You build flexibility, emotional and physical stamina, on and off the mat.

Journaling is a must. Take the time to buy a journal and favorite writing pen. Your journal does not have to be fancy. It can be a spiral notebook or a sketchbook. It needs to feel just right though, or you won't write in it. Maybe you write best on the computer. That's perfectly fine. (You may want to protect your writing with a password.)

Try this journaling exercise: put your pen to paper and write as fast as you can for five minutes. Create an evening or morning routine of writing as part of what nurtures you. You don't have to do anything with what comes up in your writing. Right now you are discovering and uncovering.

You might find these five-minute writing sprints and journal prompts helpful:

> This is my Moment of Reckoning!
>
> What in my life isn't working right now?
>
> What is working?
>
> What does my soul know that no one else knows?
>
> If I told the truth...
>
> Who am I?
>
> Who am I really?
>
> What do I know for sure?

What do I really, really know for sure?

Where do I go from here?

Where is the best place to start?

What if...?

I'm scared...

I'm excited...

I'm pretending...

If I were a Warrior Goddess, I would...

I choose me...

If I put myself first, I would...

What do I need to do to move forward?

I accept the reality of my situation, which is...

Here's the truth...

My Soulfire Woman says...

My Soulfire Woman flame just ignited...!

I'm standing in my power...

Make full use of the guided imagery available to you on my website (soulfirewoman.com). There are also apps and YouTube videos out there offering visualizations that use your imagination to heal. With guided imagery you use all of your senses as you visualize different scenes, connecting your mind and body. When you imagine with your senses, your body does not know that what you are seeing in your mind's eye isn't real, and reacts automatically. You can test this now by imagining that you are biting into your favorite piece of fruit or a lemon and seeing what happens. My salivary glands are reacting to the sour lemon as I write this. Guided imagery can calm you, reduce your anxiety, help you get to sleep, make you heal faster after surgery, develop your inner sense of knowing and heal you in a transformative way. Your imagination is the limit as to what it can do for your well-being.

Cultivate moment-to-moment awareness. Stop periodically throughout the day and say, "In this very moment, right here, right now, this is what I know to be true." Press pause and ask yourself, "What am I thinking or feeling in this moment?" You are only noticing, not making judgments or taking action. Just notice. It's important to note here that you are not your feelings or your thoughts. What you think and feel are not necessarily fact or true. They are your perceptions. Acknowledge and allow them. That's it.

Use all of your senses to bring yourself into the present moment: taste, touch, smell, sight and sound. Life itself, truly living, happens only in the present moment. Let it come alive for you. You can even isolate your senses. For example, notice only what you see by looking at how many shades of green you see, and so on. Devote some time to this practice. Being present is part of not being in your story.

Meditate. If focusing is difficult for you, begin with candle gazing. Light a candle, and soften your focus and gaze. Anchor yourself in meditation by focusing on a word that has juice for you (such as peace). Or follow your breath; notice the coolness going in and warmth going out. You can count your breath four to six counts in, hold for two at the top of the breath, and exhale for six to eight counts. This is a calming breath.

You have two minds, one who thinks and another who witnesses. You are cultivating the witness, the observer. This goes with the concept "you are not your thoughts or feelings." You are the one watching and observing your thoughts and feelings. As thoughts and feelings come up in meditation, notice and imagine them floating away as if down a stream. Then come back to your focus word or counting your breaths. Your thoughts will continue to come up. Your mind is doing what it is supposed to do, think, so you will not be able to turn this off completely, nor should you try. What will happen over time is the gap between your thoughts will widen. In the gap is where you will find answers and inspiration. Labeling your thoughts and feelings helps lessen their hold on you and helps you know just where your thoughts are going. For example, you could notice a thought and label it relationship, work, stress, and so on. Start with five minutes of meditation and work your way up to 20. Then maybe 20 minutes twice a day. No hurry here. Do what works.

Be in nature as often as possible. It is grounding, nurturing and helps you begin to know that everything in life is connected.

Dyanne Kelley

Think and translate in metaphors. See everything as symbol. Bring it into your writing. If a red cardinal comes to your window every day, what could it mean, what is it trying to tell you? If you feel a pit in your stomach or lump in your throat, what does it mean? Healing and answers will come to you this way. Journal about it with a five-minute writing sprint.

Do your best to try and make all of these a routine part of your life. Please don't worry if all doesn't come together at once. It will take time. You will gravitate to some things and not to others. That's OK. Practice here going with your gut. Do what works.

Know What You Know: From Truth-Telling to Intuition

This is what I now know: As long as there are secrets you will not heal.

Reveal and Heal

LIFE BEGAN AGAIN IN NEW ENGLAND. We started with a new counselor (one of my conditions), who met with us separately for a long time before bringing us together for marriage counseling. I don't remember exactly what I shared with him, but I must have shared a great deal. He finally brought us together for our first session. The therapist asked my husband to first admit the affair to me as a way of starting with the truth. He flat-out said, "No. I have absolutely no intention of sharing anything about that."

Incredulous, the therapist actually got angry with him, the one and only time I've ever seen a therapist do this. It was, in fact, very therapeutic for me in the moment. The therapist tried a different tactic, which also did not work. Of course, I willingly shared openly. Out of frustration, the therapist abruptly ended the session and suggested we go back into individual therapy and try marriage counseling again later. I agreed. My husband did not. The balance of power switched again. I bore my hurt silently, an invisible cloak, the weight of it taking me down, down deeper. No working through this together. He came back, after all. What else did I want?

Using Your Intuition

In my next session, the therapist asked me my assessment of a number of things regarding my relationship, husband, past, and life in general. He was very thorough and direct in his questioning.

At some point he looked at me and said, "Dyanne, why did you negate your intuition?"

"What?"

"Your intuition. Why did you discount it, ignore it? You were absolutely right on just about everything."

"Intuition, negate it? Right about everything?"

I didn't even know intuition was a method of discernment back then. I didn't know it was an innate tool I could use and rely on. This was a defining moment of grace for me. He told me I was right. That I could trust myself. Up until then, whenever I shared my feelings or my hunches, they were dismissed.

I thought I was obviously so wrong and way off. I allowed my husband and others to dismiss me. My husband wasn't comfortable in the world of feelings, although he's actually a very feeling person, so he dismissed them, his and mine. It made me feel small and emotionally unstable. To get him to listen to me, to react, I would have to escalate and create drama, making me feel out of control. Then *I* became the problem. A clever tactic used all too often in relationships where the woman often expresses herself through feelings and the male negates this approach, sticking to what seem like rational thoughts. This is also true in the workplace when women approach problems differently than men, especially when women use intuition in the solution.

Dismissed. Not heard. Now I was being told I had been right all along by an objective person, an authority figure, no less.

The counselor looked at me intently and asked me, "What do you think you will do about your marriage?" I didn't really know. He believed I had the tools to be all right should I make the decision to leave. He believed in me. I think he was silently willing me on. Whether I went back or we talked more, I don't remember. What I do remember is that I never doubted my intuition ever again. It became my guiding light, my one true source in which I believed 100 percent. It was the first thing I trusted.

My healing continued. I felt I had invested and made the commitment to stay in the marriage and stay I would, for now, at least until I got ahold of myself. It took just as much courage to stay as it did to leave, I came to realize. I started writing in a journal. I spent time with my daughter. I dabbled at various jobs, still trying to get my footing before making a final decision. I sold Mary Kay, got a real estate license, and started my Authentic Amish Quilt business, none of which really took off. I still hadn't found my thing. I took classes, trying to broaden my experiences. Nothing clicked. I decided I would go back to school and waited until we made a permanent move back to Pennsylvania. What would I go back to school for, exactly? Well, I had always wanted to be a teacher. That required certification. I thought I would be better off with a master's degree. How about school counseling? I finally decided on teaching. It would take less time, and I could get into the workforce more quickly. On three separate occasions I made an appointment with the department chair who needed to approve my courses. All three times, he did not show. The last time, I said to myself, "This is not meant to be."

I promptly walked out of the building, hiked across campus, and signed up for the counseling program. Just in time—interviews were the following week. This was synchronicity. Everything flowed into place. Interview? Check. Acceptance into the program? Check. Classes scheduled? Check.

When you are in the flow, it's a sign you are in the right place doing the right thing. This was one of those moments, when I look back, where I felt like my life was surely divinely guided. I've encountered many of these moments since, where I was forcing my sheer will on things, feeling frustrated at the lack of forward movement. And then, presto, a new door opened suddenly at Divine right timing. Walk. Through. The. Door.

I needed a graduate assistantship to pay for college. Synchronicity and fate intervened again. The only assistantship available was in the University Counseling Center. The Director there preferred all of the graduate assistants to major in college counseling. I told him I was undecided and leaning toward school counseling. I really wanted the assistantship. He hired me but continued to pressure me into choosing college counseling as a major. As it turned out, I loved working there. I declared college counseling as my major. You must understand this was not practical in any way. There were certainly many public schools in the area where I could work. There was only one small college that lent any possibility of a job following graduation. The larger colleges required doctorates. I loved the work, though, so I nervously went with it. This was probably the first time I chose out of desire and not what I thought I should do, what would be practical or make me the most money. My first career I chose for money and was so very unhappy. When you choose your passion, you create an energetic force like an invisible jet stream propelling you forward. Trust this.

Because I had arrived on the scene so late, there were only two classes not filled. One was an Intro to Theory class and the other Marriage and Family Counseling. The first was taught by a professor in a temporary, two-year position. He also worked in the counseling center. The other class was an elective and meant to be taken last in the program. They agreed to let me in the class in order to fill it and make it a go for the professor teaching it. This all felt divinely guided. The counseling program was a traditional, accredited program that dictated the types of classes and what was taught in each. But this temporary professor was determined to give us more. He wanted to make sure we were introduced to Carl Jung and the analytical theory of individuation. I had already experienced first-hand Jung's theory of synchronicities. He also theorized about the collective unconscious—inherited, universal archetypes (images and symbols) and instincts, like an encoded memory bank from all of humanity since the beginning of time. Understanding these archetypes is a knowing, a sense, a feeling, that comes from somewhere outside of our own experiences, which we relate to and automatically understand like the Goddess as mother, healer, nurturer, lover, Earth. It easily explains why so many women are currently taking to alternative forms of healing and becoming Reiki masters, aromatherapists, and naturopathic doctors. We *remember* a time when we were the healers, and our Divine Feminine gifts were revered and sought after, before the patriarchy burned our kind as witches and forced the Goddess underground. We are at a tipping point where the veil is lifting and women are increasingly remembering who we are and reclaiming our

Divine Feminine Power. Jung validated my existence. There is so much more to Jung that made me feel like I had come home: the interpretation of dreams, the persona (how we present to the world), specific personality types (Myers-Briggs Type Indicator), the anima/animus (female part of the male psyche/male part of the female psyche), the shadow side of personalities (the part of ourselves we ignore, deny and project onto others), art therapy and the spiritual. I took to Jung's theories instantly. They were a godsend and influenced how I looked at everything from that point forward. I will forever be indebted to this temporary professor who made a lasting impression on me and changed the trajectory of my life.

What's Past is Not Past—Yet

In the marriage and family class we first started by creating a genogram, a visual family psychological history going back three generations, depicting communication styles, behavioral patterns, roles, rules, and events like divorce, suicide, and so on. This required that I begin asking questions about my family, digging into family secrets. My parents divorced when I was 2, and my father was an alcoholic, according to my mom. I never saw him again really. I saw the back of him when I was 11 and officially adopted by my stepdad. My father didn't turn around to face me. I could see we had the same build and dark, wavy hair. My husband wondered why I never tried to make contact with my father. I guess it sort of felt like a closed adoption. I didn't want to disrespect my mom and stepdad, and my mom wouldn't approve, I was sure.

I knew now, being in this class, how important it was to know my history. I started asking questions and made the decision, as an adult, to seek out my biological father. I wanted to know. I was finally ready to know. My mom and her sisters were gathered for a game of pinochle, a favorite pastime. I chose that time to ask how I could find my dad, feeling safety in numbers. There was silence. My aunt broke the silence. "Well, Dyanne, I thought you knew he died a long time ago."

I couldn't breathe. I felt like I was punched in the stomach. This part of me, this choice, the ability to know the person who gave me life, was taken away from me in one fell swoop. I would never know him. I wanted to know him. I wanted to know all about him. I knew I was less like my mom's Pennsylvania German side of the family, fair-skinned, blonde, more about work than play, life as obligation, although I definitely had and respected this part of me.

But I knew in my soul I was more like my Irish side of the family. In fact, on occasion my aunts would tell me, "You're just like your father." Now I would never know. This is where my initial abandonment wound occurred, a severed relationship with my father at age 2 and again in my mid-30s. I was crushed.

Many years later I did get to meet my father's family. We had decided to go to Ireland, and unbeknown to me, my husband started to research my Irish family roots until he actually found my deceased father's relatives in Pennsylvania. He worked in Washington D.C. at the time, and instead of coming straight home one day, he drove into the mountains of Pennsylvania, planning to meet with a woman who knew the history and genealogy of that area. As he tells it, it was a foggy day, and the drive was stressful. He gave the woman my father's name. She said she not only remembered him but knew his best friend, who happened to be in town that day from Arizona visiting a bar he owned, one my father had often frequented. My husband drove to the bar, the location and dinginess of it almost keeping him from going inside. Gathering up his nerve, he went inside and asked for my father's friend. The female bartender rapped on a drainpipe with the end of an umbrella and yelled through the ceiling that there was a man there to see him.

"Tell him to come upstairs!" he yelled back. My husband went outside and climbed the rickety stairs to the second floor of the building. The place was filled with piled newspapers and dirty dishes. The friend motioned for my husband to sit down, which he did hesitantly, he said. The friend, an old man now, proceeded to share all the memories he had of my father and me as a small child. He told my husband he knew where my dad's sisters lived side-by-side. He picked up the phone and called them. My aunt started screaming on the phone that they found me. She said it was the moment they had been waiting for all of their lives, that they had been looking for me all this time. They did not realize at the time I wasn't actually physically there. My husband went to their homes, where they sat for hours talking about my dad, me, and life in between. He came away with pictures and stories.

He arrived home late that night saying he worked late. I thought he was acting odd, which roused my suspicions. Nothing seemed apparent, although I was wary. A few weeks later, on Mother's Day, I was sitting outside sipping coffee in the sunshine, still in my robe. My husband nervously presented me with a photo album complete with the story of how he found my family and what they shared. I opened the first page to a picture of my father as a child and stared into my own eyes. Healing happened in that moment, seeing my reflection in those eyes. My eyes welled up with tears as I tried to comprehend what was happening. I had found my place in the world. As he explained it, my husband was uncertain of how I would react since I had never tried very hard to find my family myself, which he never understood. Synchronicity, Divine orchestration and timing were all at play here. To me it was a miracle.

We arranged to meet after that—my new family and me. It was surreal for them. It was unreal for me. Apparently, I look, act and breathe like their brother, my father. They couldn't stop staring at me and watching me. They shared with me the ways in which I was so similar to my dad. We both ate peas and not corn. We both loved tomato jelly. We held our eating utensils the same way. We had quick wits.

My heart healed even more in that moment. I couldn't know my dad but could know about him and how much like him I am. I found a place where I fit. It felt like a final cog placed in the wheel of my existence. This story is sacred to me—mystical, magical, one that takes my breath away every time I tell it and fills me with gratitude. It was also a salve to the not-quite-healed wound of our marital relationship, with love, redemption and forgiveness seeping in. My husband and I repaired our relationship, mended our trust, and moved on with our lives together.

Telling Yourself the Truth, the Whole Truth, From the Beginning

There was more to me than my family history that needed healing. For our final project in the marriage and family class, we had to write the story of our lives, in detail. I had secrets. Stories I never told anyone. I put them all down on paper. Revealing, telling the whole truth for the first time was an emotionally cathartic moment. I could feel healing happening as my emotional cell door unlocked. This is what I now know: As long as there are secrets you will not heal. You must tell yourself the truth. It does not mean you have to do anything about your truth at the present moment. Remember, it can be your silent truth. Acknowledging it is key. Write it down and then destroy it if you must, but write it down. There's an integration that happens when your thoughts go from your head and onto your paper. Your truth is ever-unfolding as you move into deeper awareness. It has layers. What you know tomorrow or next month or next year or five years from now, you may not know today. You don't have to know it all at once. The truth will not kill you. It may feel like crap. It may be ugly. You may not like it. It's the only way.

I would like to say my great reveal was handled professionally by my professor; however, this was not the case. She was so shocked that the person who sat in her class for a semester was the same person in this paper. She thought I should have counseling. She wasn't sure if I should continue in the program. I was so good at being the perfect person that no one caught on that I might have had a troubled past. It's like an anorexic whose disease is overlooked because she is getting straight A's in school. "She couldn't possibly have problems if she is doing that well." I can look back now and know my professor was looking out for the program, assessing my ability to be a good therapist. The fight in me kicked in. I wasn't going to let anyone take this away from me. I went back underground. It wasn't safe to share. I definitely needed to be more discerning about this.

I knew that my past was something I had to deal with to move forward. I started counseling just for me with a wonderful therapist to whom I will always be thankful. I met unconditional acceptance for the first time. I wasn't treated like I had something wrong with me. I was given respect for my insight, intuition, strength and courage. It wasn't easy. I learned I had to feel to heal—to experience my feelings in a deeper way. It's important to know feelings are not the enemy. They are the key to releasing all that's locked inside of you. Transformational healing takes place on a cellular level. You have what's called a cellular memory located in every part of your body. Your body remembers what your mind may not.

All organisms within your body talk to one another, the communication frequency being your emotions moving on an internal highway of sorts. Healing is visceral regardless of the method you use to get there.

I was surviving and working on thriving. I now had an understanding as to why I feared abandonment, why I didn't feel worthy, and why I had molded myself into the "perfect" person. This was the beginning of my healing journey. It was a beginning. I still had a long way to go.

And thrive I did. I excelled in school. My confidence and sense of self-worth grew. I say all I ever needed to learn in graduate school I learned in that first semester with those first two classes. It took me forever to read my textbooks because I applied each and every line to myself, my family, my life in general. I absorbed it all and applied it. I changed. "If I can do this," I thought, "I can do anything." And about that small college down the road, the only possibility of a job close by? That's exactly where I went to work.

Here's what happened. My marriage changed because I changed. At first, I truly felt like my husband tried to downplay my success, which was really about keeping his own power. When he experienced my new sense of strength and saw how determined I was becoming with my new knowledge, I think he realized he didn't have the power over me he once had. By the time I graduated, he was very proud of me and my achievements. He respected me. More importantly, *I* respected me. I shared everything I learned, which he enjoyed hearing. A whole new world opened for both of us. When the mother grows, everyone in the family benefits, a ripple effect.

I got my power back—for real this time. I began the process of separating my identity from his and forming my own. I started school to get a career that would give me independence and, if needed, enable me to leave my marriage. I ended school with a career and a marriage. I didn't change him. *I changed. This is important.* We were actually happy for a good many years. Enough years to raise our daughter in a happy home.

Soulfire Woman Principles

You are beautiful. You were born beautiful and whole, a creation of this magnificent Universe and in the likeness of her cosmic exquisiteness. This is your birthright. Don't ever doubt this. Remember who you are.

Intuition is one of your many gifts as a Soulfire Woman. You are innately good at this. Trust in it.

Assertiveness is not a dirty word. It does not mean you are a b**ch, although if you want to be you certainly can be. You can be kind and direct at the same time. Truth-telling is not intended to deliberately hurt others. What you need and want is very important, stated clearly with intention. This is assertiveness. No one is going to look out for you like you are. That is an unrealistic expectation. Assertiveness is a balance of female and male energies. Do not confuse it with aggressiveness.

The Heroine's Journey is one of going deep within, awakening your inner knowing and strength, defining who you are at the level of your soul, and stepping out onto a new horizon with your authentic Divine Feminine Power. You shed facades, old roles that no longer fit, and overcome the seemingly impossible. In so doing you benefit yourself, your family and all those who feel the ripple effect of your courage, growth and change. This is how you help those you love and others in your energy field, not by being their caretaker for life. Being their lifelong caretaker sets you up to take care of others whose needs over time become more powerful than yours. You lose yourself in the process.

Spiritual Lessons

Synchronicities, or meaningful coincidences, are Spirit's way of illuminating the way for you. They help you make decisions and let you know you are on the right path. Once you open your eyes to synchronicities, you see them everywhere. Be on the lookout, like when you think of someone and he or she calls out of the blue, or a random person without prior knowledge starts talking with you about a life decision you're about to make, or when you want to go on a women's retreat and a flyer arrives that day announcing the perfect gathering happening soon. These are confirmations for you to guide you on your way.

There is Divine timing. It works on your behalf. Be patient. Things happen when they are supposed to and not a minute sooner.

Spiritual End Block. I truly believe there are times when I am headed in the wrong direction and just because I am so headstrong and hell-bent on making things happen, Spirit has to throw a block and change my course like it did when I thought I wanted to be a school counselor only to find that door shut tightly. Listen when this happens.

Spirit is the energy of God, Goddess, the Universe; however you define it. It also works on your behalf. Soul is that untouched part of you that connects with Spirit. This is how I experience it. Others may have a different experience or interchange the two.

Your wishes and desires are Spirit's way of laying out a path for you. You were born with them, like a homing device. Follow your passion. Your passion will lead you home to you.

When Spirits calls, go. No questions asked.

Psychological Truths

Psychology is the fast track to spirituality. If you want to be more spiritual, do your psychological work. When you grow in one, you grow in the other. I personally think the two can't be separated.

There are no spiritual bypasses for psychological issues. Adopting a yogic lifestyle or adhering to rules of organized religion, claiming the truths of those paths, does not give you a pass to skip your emotional work. Saying an empty, "I forgive you," because you are following religious teachings is very different than feeling true forgiveness in your heart. Remember—the body knows the truth. You will still feel the effects of your unresolved issues until you do the work.

You can only change yourself. Truly. This is how change happens for those connected to you. Families and relationships are like thermostats. The family sets the temperature at 72. Then you come along and bump it up to 76 (you are changing). The system works hard at bringing you back to a comfortable temperature, one the family likes, where you don't change. The system does not like change. You persist. You are too cold and want the temperature at 76. This is when change happens. The system, the family, the relationship, will either agree to the new temperature or not. They will either change with you (the best scenario), keep the temperature the same and resist, or shut down. It's a risk. You have to be willing to risk it all to create change at a systemic level. You need courage and strength to persist. When you are saving your soul, it's well worth the risk. Remember, when you change, it benefits the consciousness of the collective.

You have to feel to heal. No way around it. Feelings move like an energy highway through your body. Sometimes there are detours and roadblocks. The more you are in tune with your body, the more you will figure this out for yourself. The only way is through. Start with acknowledging your feelings. This is healing in and of itself. Even if you change how you think about something, you are still changing how you feel.

Change can happen in an instant, but usually takes more work. Give yourself time. In the spiritual world time does not exist as we know it. The Universe has its own time line, and gives you information on a need-to-know basis.

Letting go of expectations is another way of allowing versus forcing your will. Just as accepting is not resignation, letting go of expectations is not floundering aimlessly in the wind. You still set intentions or goals. You just don't hang onto the outcome. Chances are your outcome will not be as expected anyway. You may, in fact, be very surprised.

The more internal space you clear (freeing emotional blocks), the more room for your authentic Soulfire Woman to come through loud and clear, and the more power you have to live a self-directed life. You will also begin to hear your intuitive voice more often.

Do you see how we are already beginning to loop back, tying body, mind and soul together?

Dyanne Kelley

Torching Your Past

Make sure your support systems are in place. Are you practicing what nurtures you?

Go out into the night sky and pick a star. It's your star forever. It's your true north. Name it. You were born of this star. You have the same light coursing through you. Let it come in from the crown of your head all the way through the soles of your feet, anchoring and grounding you. Let it expand around you. Shine bright.

Intuition is your guiding light. As far as I'm concerned, it's an exact science once you find your way of knowing. Where do you feel your intuition? Is it in your heart, your stomach, or solar plexus? Is it just a sense you have? Ask yourself a question you want an answer to, drop from your head into the place where you feel your intuition and wait for an answer. It may come in the form of a symbol, phrase, color or complete answer. Be patient. It will come. Or maybe it comes to you in your writing. Ask yourself a question and look for symbolic answers or answers that just happen to pop up as you go about your day. Practice. Trust it.

Practice trusting your gut. Gut instincts are like instant messaging. Stay with your first impression. When your head says one thing and your gut another, go with your gut. If you're about to do something, and you feel a pit in your stomach, back away. Stop talking yourself out of things or second-guessing.

Develop a feeling language. When asked how you feel, and you answer with what you are thinking instead, this is a clue you are out of touch with your feelings. There are many more feelings in addition to happy, sad, angry, afraid and frustrated. Maybe you feel disappointed, discouraged, anxious, guilty, or confident, ecstatic, or surprised. Feelings can be very nuanced or go directly to the core of your issues. Stop and ask yourself throughout the day, "What am I feeling?" Your feelings and where you feel them lead you to your unconscious voice, that part of you that knows exactly what is right for you. When you give your unconscious voice permission to tell you the truth, your core issues will rise to the surface, often with instructions on how to heal, move forward and what to do next.

Go online and find a Myers-Briggs Personality test or something similar, like a Keirsey Temperament Sorter. Then read about your personality type. It will help you know who you are, validate this for you, and help you to understand others in your relationship circle.

Create a genogram. Go back three generations. The rules by which your family lives, overt and covert, will be revealed to you as will your roles, family myths, and even perhaps your own personal myth. You may find the clues here to your own core issues. Once you know the cycles and the patterns, you can break them. Instructions for doing this can easily be found online.

Write for four consecutive days, 15-20 minutes at a time, about things you don't really want to think about or secrets you have never acknowledged or talked about with anyone. James Pennebaker, Ph.D. used this method with college students while conducting research about the healing powers of journal writing. He found in his studies numerous health improvements over time by those who journaled, although at first report students said they felt psychologically and even physically worse. You may feel what you write on a deep level, which may not initially feel very good. However, in the integration of taking your unspoken thoughts and feelings and putting them on paper, you are preparing the way for your body, as a storehouse, and your mind, as the lock, to release what you've been holding. Your body, mind and soul will thank you for it. Depending on what you've been keeping under lock and key, you might need psychological support for this. You may choose to do whatever you want with your writing; for example, burn it, throw it away, or date and keep it. If you do dispose of it, do it with deliberate intention—make a ritual of it.

Create a "My Story" time line. This is a list of significant things in your life, turning points or events that greatly affected you and catapulted you in a certain direction, positive or negative. Under each one, write how you were feeling at the time. Look for patterns, feelings or wounds that emerged from these points in your life. Journal it, create it in art, grieve it, release it, celebrate it. Acknowledge the impact and power of each of these stepping stones in creating your present life.

Write your life story. All of it. Every detail. Now go back and rewrite it, narrating only the positive aspects of your life. Feel the difference.

Trust. There's a lot of trust happening in this process. If you have been traumatized, if you suffer from anxiety and depression, if you are not accustomed to handing over outcomes to Spirit, trust is a scary thing. Acknowledge where you are in the process. Start building trust in yourself first, then in Spirit. As I said, my intuition was the first thing I trusted. A God who was external was very difficult for me to trust. It was not until I realized an internal experience of God(dess) that I began to have faith and trust. Build a little bit at a time. Trust your intuition in small ways. For example, decide what to eat by how your body feels when you think about certain foods. Keep it small. Keep it simple. Trust that you are capable, that the answers are available to you, whether through your own intuition or Spirit, which many believe are one and the same. Ask questions; listen. Begin to build a trust circle of unconditional love. Often this begins with a therapist, a female gathering, a healing group or a spiritual/church family. Trust and unconditional love are connected. When you feel unconditional love, your ability to trust will grow, and so will your healing.

Start working with your dreams. Your dreams can be prophetic and connect you to a higher realm of knowing. Most of the time, your dreams help you solve the problems at hand and work out your daytime problems in symbolic form. They give you clues to your psychological issues. Try to remember your dreams and write them down in as much detail, using all of your senses, as you can. Pay particular attention to how you felt in each part of your dream. Now think about any anxiety or stress you might have felt during the day, and if the dream helps you work that out in a symbolic way. At bedtime you can even ask for your dreams to help you work some things out or for an answer to a particular question.

PART II:
IGNITING YOUR PRESENT

Feel To Heal: Good Grief

There are stories we tell ourselves, stories we keep hidden, stories we tell others.

MY INNER WORK WAS ALL PREPARATION for what was to come. I was managing life just fine, although I was stressed as a working mom. Then I had the brilliant idea of having an exchange student for a year. In my infinite wisdom I thought she would be good for my daughter, who loved and looked up to older kids and was not quite old enough to stay by herself after school. On paper, our exchange student was perfect. She loved playing basketball, just like my daughter did. She seemed active and engaging. I suspect in hindsight she said on paper what she thought we Americans wanted to hear. I already had preconceived expectations of what this year was going to be like. The person who got off of the plane was a young woman with her naturally white-blonde hair dyed black, dressed completely in black, Goth style. In the days ahead we would find out our student had zero interest in sports of any kind, and not many interests in general. She rarely came out of her room and made only one friend, another Goth, whom we found difficult to trust. I tried to explain very gently that being Goth might be viewed differently in the U.S. than in her own country, Germany. But there was no change. She wore black head to toe every day and regularly dyed her hair in our bathtub. I worried about her well-being.

Our student communicated only with me and ignored my daughter as if the rest of the family didn't exist. My daughter quickly distanced herself, embarrassed by the young woman's Morticia look. Family activities held little interest, and she never offered to pitch in around the house with dishes or laundry, which only increased my workload and stress as a working mom. What I thought was going to be fun turned into a nightmare. Me and my good ideas. What was I thinking?

My family was not too happy with me, especially my daughter. Our home no longer felt like home with so much underlying tension, an invisible current of electricity. I was totally unprepared for this scenario. It was supposed to be fun, a great experience. I had no experience with a teenager and setting rules about curfews and who she could hang out with in general. The responsibility to make this relationship work fell on my shoulders alone. That feeling felt so familiar to me—like a line from a movie script I was already living. Here I was, doing it all, *again*. My husband traveled with his work and was available only on weekends. I thought having an international student would help transition our daughter to middle school. Instead it doubled, tripled and quadrupled my stress. I did what I did best, tried and tried and tried again to make the relationship work by bending, accommodating, being *SelfLESS*.

Stressed to my max, I sought help and intervention from the foreign exchange people, who tried to remedy the situation but got nowhere themselves. They decided after nine months to send the student home early for circumstances beyond my control. While I was seeking the agency's help, I had not expected them to make such a decisive action as sending her home. It was awful. I felt wracked with guilt. They made the decision, had her arrangements made, and sent her home within 24 hours. Talk about a 24 hours I never want to repeat. I was emotionally and physically exhausted. Did she exhaust me or did I exhaust myself? Was it her or the expectations I placed on her? If I had shifted what I thought should be to what really was, I might have saved us both a lot of heartache. At some point in life we learn that expectations, when unmet, are a setup for unpleasant feelings and actions. Imagine what would have happened if I had just accepted her as she was and loved her anyway? I did this later, by the way. I invited her, her sister and a friend back for an extended vacation. I apologized for my part in what happened. We both felt peace and a sense of closure. I also could see clearly she *was* different from her sister and friend who were both pleasant, helpful, appreciative and kind. Not that this excuses my part in the whole scenario. What I also saw clearly was how hard I tried, how hard I *always* tried to make relationships work, how as women we tend to do this at the sacrifice of our own well-being. How I took responsibility for something that maybe could not be fixed. Some things just couldn't be fixed and it wasn't my fault. It didn't mean I was flawed in some way, that I lacked something or had some deficit. I did the best I could with the situation. I could see that now. I also saw clearly how pervasive *guilt* was in my life—my heart pumping it out like blood with each beat and sending it to all my extremities. Guilty that I wasn't perfect. Shame, to be exact.

Dyanne Kelley

It was shortly after the exchange student left that I started having difficulty walking. I walked every day at lunch, a loop around campus with a hill or two. I could no longer go up the hills without huffing and puffing. The college nurse came into my office one day after I had just returned from a walk. "Something's wrong," I said. "I have no stamina. I can't breathe. Look at my legs," I said. I took off my shoes and socks and showed her my swollen feet and ankles, baby elephant legs stuck onto lily pads. She started to look panicked and insisted I immediately go to the doctor.

At the same time we were renovating our kitchen. I sat on the floor to unpack the cupboards and reached up to the counter to pull myself up. I couldn't stand up on my own. I couldn't go up and down the stairs to do the laundry. I was sleep deprived, sweating, tossing and turning. My heart pounded out of my chest. I felt old, very old. I paced, feeling anxious and alert all the time. It was interesting to me that I had gotten so sick almost completely under the radar. While I repeatedly complained of a racing heart and exhaustion, that I didn't feel well and thought something was wrong, I wasn't heard. I never felt heard. My concerns were minimized by doctors and my husband. *Minimized, not heard, dismissed.* Those pesky repeated themes in my life. I martyred on, completely taking apart the kitchen and setting up an alternate kitchen in another room. I did dishes in the bathtub. I cooked on the grill or in the microwave. I went without sleep.

And no one noticed. No one read my mind. No one tried to lift the burden. No one blinked an eye. Being a martyr was not the solution. I only got sicker.

Tests, tests, and more tests. Finally, the diagnosis came: Graves' disease, hyperthyroid. I was immediately put on medications that slowed my heart rate and helped me sleep.

I was told the only treatment was radioactive iodine to kill the thyroid, resulting in a hypothyroid condition. I sought more opinions. All the same. I desperately tried to figure out an alternative to killing off my thyroid and could find none. My heart was at risk, they said. I knew nothing of mind/body healing then. Doctors scared me into believing I had to take quick and swift action, or I could suffer heart damage. Now they were listening, now that blood tests confirmed how sick I was. I finally relented, and agreed to the treatment.

I began to grieve. I grieved the loss of my ability to regulate my own body. My eyes bulged. I developed a goiter. I couldn't get enough to eat, feeling hungry all day long. I actually gained weight, which is usually not the case with hyperthyroid. My once bouncy, curly hair went limp and dry. I relied on a pill, something synthetic to make my body function as it should. There was no family history that I was aware of for hyperthyroid. "Stress," the doctors said. "Exchange student," I thought.

Can You Hear Me Now?

I knew in my heart it went deeper than that—beyond the stress of a year with an exchange student. She was the catalyst. It was not lost on me that my illness was in my throat, swollen with my silence, too many things left unsaid, the source of my shame. Insight alone was the first step in my healing. Now there were things I needed to say and people in my past I needed to say them to. I knew instinctively I had to find my *voice*.

This is the thing about hyperthyroidism. For some reason you lose your filter. Maybe it was because I was so sick at the time, I didn't care. Maybe I was just sleep deprived. All I knew was I couldn't hold things inside any longer. It was making me sick. My past came right into the present and choked me. All the secrets I held inside created a fireball and exploded like a volcano. I spewed everywhere. *The voice* came out, shattering my silence. I needed to let those who hurt me as a child know I remembered the sexual abuse, all of it, that just because I was seemingly OK, I still dealt with haunting memories and fears. I wrote detailed letters and sent them certified, letters I knew I could never take back. I felt relieved of the straightjacket binding me so tight. No more secrets. I can't remember if I expected some form of admission, an acknowledgment of pain and suffering, an apology. None of those showed up for me. Blaming me, the victim, is what showed up on my doorstep like an uninvited guest. I felt victimized all over again. No one said "I believe you." There was no talking it out, no wound tending or healing. Relationships abruptly came to a halt. I was somewhat ready for it though, having subconsciously prepared for this moment for a long, long time. Not that it didn't hurt. But the other way hurt more, pretending I was fine, keeping up an illusion so others could feel better, putting their well-being before my own, tending to relationships.

Doing the right thing is no guarantee of a pain-free life. You may feel worse before you feel better, and I did feel worse for a long while. The hard part had been maintaining those relationships over the years as if they were normal and nothing at all had happened. I wonder why I did that. I don't have a clear answer except that it became a way of life for me; the only way I knew how to survive. I do know in my childhood these were things we just did not talk about to anyone. We only endured becoming martyrs as a way of survival. My silent martyrdom worked for a while until my body proclaimed loudly and clearly, "Enough of this." Your mind is never smarter than your body. Let me say that again. Your mind is *never* smarter than your body. Learn to listen very closely to what your body has to say.

There are stories we tell ourselves, stories we keep hidden, stories we tell others.

At some point you need to get on the elevator and press the button for the ground floor, where you can find the story beneath the story, the truth waiting for you right there, the foundation on which you build your life. The truth, while having its consequences, helped me begin to unravel the intricate network of exhausting survival skills I had been using to present myself as normal, pretending to be perfect, never getting angry, emotionally manipulating not to be abandoned, drinking too much to keep the memories at bay, living life rigidly, thinking I could handle remaining silent like it didn't matter to my body or soul. Being abused isn't the most important part of the story here. It's what I did with that story, how I tried to erase it with maladaptive behaviors and lost sight of myself in the process. It was like ripping off a page of a tablet you have recently written on. The next page looks seemingly blank, like free space, but if you take the side of a pencil to it you can read it just as clearly. Your subconscious always knows the truth.

I raised the temperature on the thermostat, then insisted and persisted it not be lowered again. My Soulfire burned strong now, refusing to be extinguished. Telling the truth was like a key opening up all the locked doors to the hidden rooms inside me. I felt strong and empowered by standing up for myself. I was now free to be me—to remember who I was before the layers of inauthentic, fake identities made me forget.

You and I know that women silence themselves all too often. Swallowing our truths puts us at the mercy of someone else who then holds all our power.

Finding your voice, learning to say what is true, is necessary to stepping into your Soulfire Woman Power. Say what is true even if it's just to yourself. Ask for what you need. Make your opinions known. Being stoic gets you nowhere. Nowhere. Trust me. Please know that I am definitely not recommending that you take a similar path. There are ways of dealing with your past that do not require direct confrontation or such extreme measures. This is where a qualified psychotherapist can help you.

Good Grief

The hurt turned into a grief like nothing I ever felt before. I grieved for the little girl in me, for the lost innocence, for the healthy relationships I never had. One of the most powerful things I did for myself was inner child guided visualizations. I met myself as a little girl, but now *I* was the adult caring for her, telling her what to look out for and what to expect in life. I *loved* her. I welled over with love for her. It triggered something inside of me. I felt sorry for myself. I wallowed. I wailed. I cried. I mourned. I got angry. I got sad. Then I did it all over again, another layer, then another.

Until one day I got up, wiped away my tears and got on with my life. I was done grieving and feeling sorry for myself. It felt like a major step in healing was completed. It was time to *be*. Allowing myself to grieve healed me down deep into my bones to my cells—this I knew for sure. Like a waterfall of tears, it washed me clean and let me begin again. It will be necessary for you too, whether you are grieving divorce or children going away to college or unresolved trauma. It is *good grief.* Get on with it. You have to feel to heal. My emotional strength regained, I was ready to dig deeper.

Soulfire Woman Principles

Being a Soulfire Woman and a martyr are not the same. One wields power from strength within. The other emotionally manipulates by sacrificing herself to feel her power.

Your voice is strong, unwavering and powerful. Own it. Do not accept silence, unless your life is in danger, as a way to make those around you feel better, to be a *nice* girl and not rock the boat, and/or to avoid stepping into your own power.

Soulfire Women do not whine or complain. Soulfire Women identify, deal with and solve problems using collaboration and consensus.

Spiritual Lessons

Asking for help is a strength, not a weakness. Ask your soul friends, ask your angels, guides, God(dess), the Holy Spirit. It means you recognize where there's a hole in your soul, where your consciousness is unable to help you, that you need another means of knowing from your unconscious, higher self, and other spiritual dimensions. Be specific about what you are asking and how you want to know the answer. Not asking only hurts you in the end by keeping all of that hurt inside, blocking your ability to see clearly. All of our saints implored for help and understanding in what they called the dark night of the soul. Trust. Wisdom will come.

Life events are opportunities for spiritual lessons, teaching you, bringing you to wisdom and understanding. My exchange student taught me that I lived with expectations, I was a caretaker above and beyond, I was a relationship fixer to my own detriment, and that I lived with guilt and shame. Pretty powerful lessons.

The mind, body and soul are connected. As soon as you think something, your body feels it and responds in some physiological way. In fact, your body does not know if what your mind is thinking is actually happening or not. It just reacts. You experience this in your dreams. For example, if you dream you fell off a cliff, you jolt awake, your heart racing, afraid you might be dying.

Grieving is a portal to forgiveness.

Psychological Truths

No one will read your mind, nor should you expect them to. You cannot hold others accountable for something you think they should do if you haven't actually asked them to do it. Expecting others to read your mind is something a martyr might do.

Grieving is the key to unlocking what you keep hidden inside. It is necessary to move forward. Grief includes anger. It includes wishing whatever happened had never happened to you. It has levels. You may go through it on one level and turn around and find a deeper grief you were not aware of.

One doesn't necessarily happen after the other. Months and years can go by before you reach a new level. It will happen when it's supposed to.

Every loss, no matter how small, involves grieving. Grieving can be brief, yet necessary. It can happen in a yoga session or a journal exercise or during an acupuncture treatment. It's a release of stuck energy. Stuck energy creates emotional, behavioral and physical problems.

Emotional development often gets stuck at the point in your life when trauma occurs. Say, for example, you were sexually abused at age 8 or 9. Now there is a hurt, scared little girl inside who needs rescuing, to be kept safe and secure, who may need a parent. She will live life from her little girl perspective instead of stepping into her adult self. The hurt little girl will look for someone to rescue her or parent her or even abuse her until she recognizes the pattern, grieves, heals and—with awareness—chooses differently. These patterns will repeat if not cleared or worked through emotionally.

Igniting the Present

This can be tough work. Again, make sure your support systems are in place.

Journal prompts:

>Where have I been a martyr?

>Why am I in this same relationship again?

>When/Where in my life did I get stuck?

Dyanne Kelley

> What patterns do I keep repeating?
>
> My little girl self says...
>
> My adult self says...

Use your *voice*. If you want or need something, make it clear. Ask. This is being assertive. Use "I" messages:

"When you do this_____, *I* feel _____, and *I* would like it if you could _____. Thank you for listening to my concerns."

Practice making sounds with your voice. Listen to your sounds. Sing, hum, shout. Learn yoga breathing techniques like the *hara* breath. Stand with your feet hip distance apart, positioning your weight evenly. Bend your knees slightly, reach out with your arms, make fists and pull back forcefully while making a *Ha* sound as your elbows hug your ribcage. Repeat for one minute. Make some noise. Then talk. Address your needs and concerns.

Inner child work is a great way to heal the wounded parts of yourself from childhood by connecting to the little girl within you. First acknowledge her, listen to her, and most importantly, love her. Open a line of communication by asking her opinion and how she feels. You can do this by writing her letters and letting her write back to you. Give her a voice. The first letter you write in your voice and the return in her voice. You can also dialogue with her, imagining you are talking back and forth, asking her what she most needs, what messages she might have for you, what she wishes you would have told her. Then write it down. Write a dialogue just like you are writing a movie script.

Guided imagery is specifically-directed visualization. There is guided imagery for anxiety, depression, pain, connecting with universal spirit; for anything you can imagine. Your body responds on a cellular level to imagery. It has the power to transform and heal. At Soulfire Woman, guided imagery is used as a part of healing. You can also find guided imagery online.

Unsent letters are an excellent way to help you find closure with someone you can't really talk to, like an ex or a parent. I wrote to my deceased father, letting all of my feelings spill onto the page. The point of unsent letters is to not censure yourself: talk, rage, spew profanity if you wish, directed specifically to someone in particular:

"Dear _____, What I really want you to know..."

Let it all out. You're not going to send it. It is like a confrontation without an actual confrontation. Unsent letters can also be a dress rehearsal of sorts, preparing you for when you do want to say something to someone without all of the emotions. They help you get all the emotion out first so you can say what you really want to say in a calmer, more direct, even-toned way.

Crying is cleansing. Let the salt in your tears rise up within you, wash over you and heal you. Some women have bottled up their tears for so long, they can't cry. Start with watching tear-jerker movies. Get used to your tears. Soulfire Women cry. Crying is holy.

Mind-body connection. I want to be clear here that you are not responsible for all disease that may happen to you. There are environmental, nutritional and genetic factors at play as well. However, unresolved issues do live in your body and make you sick emotionally and physically. To become more aware of your mind-body connection, you can find the physical stuckness first; for example, an aching back, and then figure out what it means symbolically or metaphorically. Or, sometimes you feel stress and know it is in your neck, or shoulders, etc. I went for years with a low backache before I realized this is where I carry my stress and my locked emotions. Always ask those hurting/aching parts of yourself what is causing the pain. You may be surprised by the answers. Sometimes it's just a lousy pillow, and other times it's a deep-seated resentment. Look for the deeper meaning.

Get Into Your Body: Connecting Mind, Body and Soulfire

My body started talking to me. Or to be more exact, I started listening.

I GRIEVED MY LOSSES, yet I was still living in my head with the intellectual understanding of my issues versus what I needed to do to heal on an even deeper level. Now it was time to go further inward. Just why had I gotten so sick? My body knew the answer, of that I was sure. My body lived and breathed my entire life history. What living proof was there for me to find?

I started reading about chakras, an ancient system for physical health, emotional wellbeing and higher consciousness. The chakras are seven energy centers in the body correlating with your nervous system and endocrine glands, which work together in balancing your psychological and physical health, connecting mind and body. When these energy centers are blocked through injury or repressed emotions, for example, physical disease can result. When they are open, we connect with universal life force and unlimited potential. It made complete sense to me. I read *Energy Anatomy* by Caroline Myss, Ph.D., a medical intuitive, and *Women's Bodies, Women's Wisdom* by Christiane Northrup, M.D., both seminal works in mind/body and women's healing. Every illness, every emotional issue connects to one or more of the seven energy centers. I intuitively knew this. I began to see my patterns, looking at my body first, then my emotions, and pieced together how my past created issues for me in the present. I had an intellectual understanding of it. I knew that abandonment was located in my first chakra, guilt, shame and emotions in my second, and lack of worthiness in my third. Now I had to get in there and feel it. Not only feel it, but transmute and transform it.

As a therapist, I began translating every issue brought to therapy through the filter of chakras, which guided me in facilitating emotional healing. The truth about being a psychotherapist is you can only take clients as far as you've gone yourself. Not that you have to experience everything a client has experienced to be helpful; you can't possibly. Whatever your issues are though, you need to work through them and continue working through them to be genuine and effective. Sometimes I was just one step ahead...

Tapping Into Your Body's Wisdom, Your Most Sacred Talent

My body started talking to me. Or to be more exact, I started listening. I was so out-of-touch at the time that I didn't even know where I held stress. I started doing body scans, mentally going over each part of my body and noticing, checking in regularly to what I was sensing in my body. I opened myself up and expanded in every possible way. It was like having a personal growth spurt.

Journal writing helped me to identify and process my feelings, to try on new ways of being on paper. I found a book about journaling called *Journal To The Self: Twenty-Two Paths to Personal Growth* by Kathleen Adams, M.A. I took the certified instructor training in Colorado, the first time I had ever been away from my husband and daughter for any length of time, and the first major training I took outside of graduate school. I got on a plane to go somewhere by myself! It was exhilarating!

I used the techniques liberally with myself and still do. I dialogued, first as an imagined then a written conversation with every aspect of myself: my lonely self, my child self, my powerful self, just about every self you can think of. I wrote character sketches of everyone in my life, alive, imaginary, and passed on, of God(dess) herself. I wrote character sketches of how everyone in my life experienced me. This was particularly helpful in showing me how others saw me, providing me with a different perspective. The not-so-glamorous part of doing this work is that you tend to become self-absorbed. Sometimes you need to bring yourself out of being the center of your own universe for just a little while. There's no doubt my husband felt neglected during this period of our marriage. That's the thing I've learned about marriage. Sometimes it's your turn to surge and sometimes it's your turn to support. Your partner will hopefully grow with you as well as you with your partner. It's when two people don't that it becomes a problem...

The trainings kept coming, only now I felt like they were finding me. While I had started a video yoga practice and practiced with some regularity, I would never call myself a yogi. Nor did I ever want to teach. Though I did feel I could help my clients by knowing more about how yoga heals. Then a yoga training appeared in which a pioneer in yoga therapy, Joseph Le Page, offered *Integrative Yoga Therapy* at an ashram a couple of hours away. It fell right in my lap. I began to feel myself being pulled, drawn, compelled to say yes to certain things like I was being told to do it without any immediately apparent reason. Synchronicity plus a push for good measure. This would happen to me more and more in my life; exercises in following my intuition. I nervously did say yes to what I affectionately called yoga boot camp. Two weeks at an ashram in Pennsylvania. Starting at 6 a.m. and ending at 10 p.m. daily, beginning with meditation, then an hour-and-a-half of yoga, half-hour breakfast, half-hour to shower, two hours of asana practice, one-hour lunch, two three-hour lectures, dinner followed by an evening program. Fall into bed. Get up and do it all over again. Two weeks. One day off. It *felt* like boot camp, breaking down my old system of being and reformulating it into a new system.

My experiential world grew larger to include breath work to balance mood; mudras, gestures of the hand, face and body promoting psychological and physical well-being and spiritual awakening; Ayurveda, the sister system of yoga, which integrates the body, mind and Spirit through a comprehensive holistic health approach; and more about the chakras. I learned that yoga offered a complete psycho-spiritual pathway to health, wellness and enlightenment.

One thing led into another. At a Caroline Myss workshop, I found books by Ron Roth, a former Catholic priest (now deceased) who had become a healer. I decided one day to follow one of his meditations on the Holy Spirit asking for guidance on what I should be doing with my life. I stated I would do whatever I was asked to do by the Holy

Spirit, that I was listening. I was instructed to breathe from my heart center. Normally I meditated with my palms down. For some reason, that day I turned them up. And then it happened. It felt like my palms had become magnets pulling in from the Universe. Something with weight and density zapped into my hands. My hands moved with the weight of it, or so it seemed. My eyes popped open. I had no words. Did that just happen? I wondered if I was imagining things. Day after day I put it to the test. This thing in the palm of my hands electrified at my beckon. You must consider that I was a traditional psychotherapist and had never heard of energy healing before in my life. It was also long before energy modalities like Reiki became household names. I thought people would think I was crazy. I told my husband and one friend. Not sure where to turn or look, I did nothing. It wasn't until two years later when a psychic, during my very first psychic reading, asked me if I did laying on of hands. I laughed and said, "No, but I have this funky thing going on with my hands." She assured me I was going to do energy healing in my future.

This legitimized it for me and gave me permission to pursue it in some way. I went to the master first, Ron Roth, and his Celebrating Life Ministries conference in Chicago. He taught that anyone can heal and be a healer; through the Holy Spirit, through prayer by clearing your past issues using your chakras, and by believing that whomever you touch is actually healed, just like when Jesus said, "You are healed." People lined up and waited their turn to be touched and healed by Roth. Stories of his miracles were being whispered and circulated through the crowd, although he was clear the miracles did not come directly from him, only through him. As conference participants, we each filed up to receive a blessing. People were "spotted" from behind, as some who received the blessing collapsed. I was skeptical, as I sometimes am. It was my turn. I walked up to him. He looked me in the eyes, placed his hand on my head and blessed me. I felt my legs buckle, nearly giving out beneath me. I swayed back to my seat and sat in awe. Whatever this thing was that just happened, I was definitely a believer.

I was a believer but did not have the confidence to try this at home. Seriously, I couldn't just say, "You ARE healed!" My ego needed more. The Omega Institute of Holistic Studies catalogue arrived in the mail, and I opened it right to Reconnective Healing, an energy healing modality, said to myself, "Hmmm... interesting," and promptly signed up. At dinner beforehand I met a few other people attending the training. Together we walked to the auditorium and took our seats in the first row. I'm not a first-row kind of gal; however, I quickly realized why I was there. Everything that was being demonstrated I could feel in my hands, which were vibrating like crazy. I took it as confirmation that this was what I was being asked to do by the Holy Spirit or God or Goddess or the Universe. I went home and opened an energy healing practice—a novel thing at the time—with a little more confidence. I advertised in the local free weekly paper and immediately started getting phone calls from people calling me a witch, among other things, and then hanging up. I was a little unnerved, although I had the firm belief that I was being guided to do this and was determined to continue. I did live in fear of losing my psychotherapy license at the time. All of this was just so new. I was careful to separate the two practices. I became the local Democrat (another charge against me) and resident witch. I kept going.

By the way, we lived in a 200-year-old Pennsylvania limestone house we were sure was haunted. We all had our own experiences in that realm. I would most often smell cinnamon and apple pie baking in the living room or cherry pipe smoke on the upstairs landing in the middle of the night. They were always comforting things to me; I never felt afraid. I was told later that the ghosts liked me because I was quiet. Good for me, I guess. My daughter saw visions of people walking through the house, appearing at the foot of her bed and in the corner of the spare bedroom. One night she saw a woman open the basement door. She wondered why I would do laundry so late at night. Then she realized the woman was wearing a long skirt, had her hair pulled up and was not holding a laundry basket. At first, I thought it was middle school drama. Then one night my daughter came screaming into the kitchen holding the cat, saying she saw a guy in the corner of the spare bedroom. She knew she saw something, she said, because the cat's tail tripled in size. The cat's tail was still huge. She hissed. I went upstairs with the two of them, and as soon as I stepped into the room, a ripple traveled up my spine through the crown of my head, making me feel like my hair was standing on end. I knew then she was experiencing exactly what she said. There was much more to life than I could see with my eyes.

All of this was certainly making me think outside of the box. I was experiencing things through my senses, through my belief in Spirit and trust in my intuition, which I would later come to know as God herself. I delved into Celtic spirituality and felt like I had found my way home. My identity was forming. And it was all about remembering who I was, who I came into the world as, not who I thought I should be. *I AM.*

Meanwhile, as a mother, the older my daughter got the more hypervigilant I became. I did not want her to suffer the same traumas I did as a child. I made strict rules. It was ridiculous to think like this, and I shouldn't be concerned about anything, they said. This is what changed. I did not let the fact that others tried to dismiss, ignore or minimize what I was saying make me doubt myself. I knew the truth. I stood my ground, I kept my power, until my daughter was old enough to make her own decisions. Then life resumed like nothing ever happened.

In my marriage, I had a lot of difficulty with trust, as you can imagine, and I had to work hard at keeping my anxiety down. Then one day I realized I had very little control over anything. I had spent my life up until that point trying to control as much as I could, to anticipate every detail in advance so that I could keep myself from more emotional pain and protect myself from hurt. It didn't work. Like all of the other defenses I had accumulated, I reached a point where this no longer did the job as intended. I needed new strategies. Knowing that there wasn't anything I could conceivably control outside of myself was a good place to start.

Soulfire Woman Principles

You are integrity and truth. Live it. It will then be impossible for anyone to deny the essence of who you are.

Truth requires action. Stepping into your Warrior Goddess is sometimes a necessary action.

Here's the truth about being minimized and dismissed. You *let* others do this to you. If you feel strong from the inside out, confident in your truth and integrity, then no one can minimize you. No one would dare.

If what you observe is real, you are not being judgmental of others. You are the purveyor of truth.

Spiritual Lessons

Chakras are a roadmap to health, psychological well-being and enlightenment.

When you receive an intuitive hit, saying yes as quickly as possible amplifies the energy of success. Thinking about it depletes the energy at its source. You lose the momentum of Universal power. Ride the energy wave!

Your ego is intended to protect you. However, when it goes into overdrive and makes all of your decisions for you, you become fear-based instead of intuitive/Spirit-based. This separates you from Spirit.

Trying to control life, other people, situations and outcomes serves only to make your life more difficult. Think about all of the energy this takes. If you let go of control and accept life as it is, only then will you gain your freedom.

We live in a Universe beyond three dimensions. There are things we can't see that are present energetically and in the invisible, which you may be able to know through feeling, touching, sensing, hearing, smelling, dreaming, seeing in images or symbols or just by knowing. Use all of these to see beyond.

Psychological Truths

You can't heal by being in your head and using rational thought. Believe me, you can rationalize anything. Also, your small mind plays devil's advocate. There isn't anything you can think that your small mind will not respond to with a, "What if...." It thinks this is its job. Well, it is really. *Only your body knows the truth.*

Anxiety does not exist on its own. It almost always has an antecedent. Figuring out what is causing your anxiety is key.

Igniting Your Present

Life sometimes requires the superhero stance. Feet are hip distance apart. Fists on your hips. Tilt your chin upward. Turn up the corners of your mouth. *Wonder Woman!*

Get out of your head. Check in with your body periodically throughout the day with quick body scans. What is your body trying to say to you? Trust this is the truth. Yoga can be helpful here. You can't stay in your head, listen to the teacher, and do the poses. You have to be present.

Anxiety can be debilitating. First figure out where in your body you feel anxiety. Ask anxiety what it is trying to tell you. Listen for the answer, then ask, "What is beneath that?" Now, "What is beneath that?" Keep going until you get to *the* answer. You should eventually come to one of your core fears like abandonment, rejection, being shamed, failure and so on.

If all of your decisions and actions are based on fear, then your ego is on overdrive trying to protect you. This can sometimes be difficult to discern. For example, you may need or want recognition or extra attention. Ask, "Why?" Your ego may be protecting you from hurt. Ask yourself, "What part of me is hurt?" It's important to figure this out. If you are in fear, you are not in love. You need to *be in love*. Before you do anything, ask yourself why you are doing it. And, "What's beneath that?"

Get to know all the parts of yourself. Recognize which parts of you need to be healed for you to move forward. Address each one by one. Know who is actually doing the talking at any given time. Is it your adult self, hurt child self or critical self? Funny girl? Wise woman? For example, if you are trying to win an argument in a relationship by coming from your child self, you may get a parental response, exactly what you probably don't want. Know which self you are operating from; this dictates the kind of response you will get from others.

Know your defenses and blind spots. What part of you are you trying to protect? What feelings cause you to become defensive? Shame, hurt, fear... these are all clues to what you need to heal. You work backward from the present to the past, noticing all the times you felt those things until you come to *it*. That's the healing space, right there.

Meditate by breathing and opening your heart to the Universe or the Holy Spirit, often interpreted as the feminine energy of God. Say you are listening and willing to do whatever is asked of you. Listen for the answer.

PART III: SETTING YOUR SOUL ON FIRE

Open Your Heart: Forgiveness, Love and Gratitude Begin with Yourself

Forgiving yourself is seismic. It is the self-love turning point, a moment of transition and transformation.

I SPENT A LOT OF YEARS BEING ANGRY—a lot of years. It was wearing and tearing me down, I knew. At one time or another I felt emotionally and physically abandoned; not supported or respected. And you know what? I survived. I didn't melt into the ground and disappear. I could live through abandonment and was OK. Life wasn't perfect, but I had my integrity. I had my grit and determination, my survival instincts. The awareness of abandonment not being the worst thing that could happen helped me begin the process of stepping out and rising up out of victim consciousness. I wanted to stand alone in my own power, another leap on the path of the Soulfire Woman's Way.

What I needed to do was focus on what was good, and there was a lot of good, and heal negative family patterns and dynamics. I observed my husband's family, a kind family who valued people's feelings. I absorbed goodness from my church family. I created my own family unit—healing in itself. We made new traditions and filled our home with love. My husband was instrumental in this as he valued the childhood traditions that he recreated. He was also a very kind and generous man who treated others with respect.

One day I realized, "You know what? No one can hurt me anymore." All of my life's dynamics had shifted. My old stories no longer mattered. I was in charge of my own decisions and choices. I couldn't be manipulated or controlled any longer. My daughter was old enough to make her own decisions. We had given her the foundation she needed to be an independent adult. No one could hurt her, either. My experience had not been her experience. She only remembered good times and love. I also could see that people do not stay the same and for the most part grow and try to be better people.

It's hard to let go of anger and hurt. There comes a point in time when it no longer serves you, a point in time when you have moved beyond it and drawing the line in the sand is no longer helpful. There is no eye for an eye unless you spend your life making that happen.

I realized it was time to let go of how I wanted things to be versus how they actually were. Things just don't happen the way you imagine. They don't happen to you. They happen for you. They happen so that you learn spiritual lessons.

I had done my job as a mother protecting my daughter. I no longer wanted to be angry about the past. I had worked through how my past was affecting me in the present, knew when I was being triggered and could, with awareness and discernment, alter my patterns. I no longer blindly acted out of fear of abandonment and shame. I created newer, healthier patterns based on honesty, integrity, kindness, love and service to others. I read Marianne Williamson's *A Return to Love* and relied on her book *Illuminata* to give me the prayers I needed at any given moment. As I peeled away the layers, I found myself. *She* was waiting there all along. And this is what I discovered: I could be myself and people didn't abandon me. They liked me for who I was and had always been. I experienced people *staying* in my life. The overarching fear of being left, of being alone, subsided.

I learned how to love without conditions. When my daughter was born, the women from the small Presbyterian Church down the road where I had been attending, although I was not yet a member, delivered seven days of meals. I mean complete meals with homemade baked bread and dessert. Up until that time, I thought it was truly the nicest thing anyone had ever done for me. They knew I had a baby because my husband hung a flag above the front door saying, "It's a Girl!" The minister visited us in the hospital when my daughter was quarantined, another nicest thing ever. Eventually I joined the church, began to teach Sunday school and years later became active as an Elder. During my time as an Elder, I learned unconditional service to others and how to lead with love. I also began to discern my own religious beliefs. *The Dance of the Dissident Daughter* by Sue Monk Kidd, the *Gnostic Gospels* by Elaine Pagels and other books helped me to formulate my beliefs. I knew this for sure: I believed in my own experience of God. I did not feel God outside of myself. I felt God inside of me, moving through me. My God definitely had a feminine face. And this is how the Soulfire Divine Feminine presents herself; you feel and embody her. She is you.

One with God(dess)

Spiritual lessons kept coming, bringing together mind, body and soul for me. One vivid lesson arrived when I was startled awake in the middle of the night by my barking dog. I was disoriented in the midst of a dream in which I was confused about what was real and what wasn't. Even upon awakening in the morning I felt upset, unsure of myself, and doubted reality. This dream really played with my mind. Why can't I figure it out? Am I really losing it?

In the dream I had done something unethical. Thinking about it now still gives me a pit in the middle of my stomach. All the fear I felt in my life manifested symbolically in this dream. I was starting to feel crazy. I began to understand how someone who is not in his or her right mind must feel. I realized how easily this line could be crossed. I couldn't calm myself. Self-talk, journaling—nothing helped. I also wasn't aware of how dreams work through your everyday anxieties in symbols. Fear literally took over my life.

Finally, an epiphany came: The only one true thing you know for sure is Spirit, who, no matter what the circumstances, will never abandon you.

There was an untouchable center of my being, my soul, directly connected to Spirit like an umbilical cord. In the midst of my confusion that bordered on craziness, I knew this for certain. It alone was my solace. I had never been alone and never would be alone ever again. Nothing else was real. Nothing.

It was a lifeline for me. Once I knew I could rely on that, and God was with me always, in me, my soul calmed, and I resumed life knowing the most important thing was staying connected with Spirit. I was literally one with God, Spirit, the Universe—a consciousness beyond myself.

Forgiveness and Love Start with Yourself

I contemplated forgiveness. I asked myself, "How do I forgive someone who hasn't asked for my forgiveness or even admitted culpability?" I thought about redemption. People do redeem themselves, like I tried to do with our international student. Not any one person is all bad or all good. Like my husband, who had betrayed my trust and yet presented me with the miraculous gifts of my daughter, my father's family and self-healing opportunities. My dream let me know how easily this line between right and wrong could be crossed. We all deserve peace of mind, I thought. People do bad things and still have a lot of good in them. People make mistakes and learn from them. Who knows, maybe my dream was intended to push me toward forgiveness. I could look at all the characters, their past and present, and understand how and why things happened the way they did. I could understand also that when a person does something so wrong, it's very hard to outwardly admit it. They rationalize to make it seem less awful. An alternative they have is to choose differently going forward and be a better person. Not everyone does this though—becomes a better person. Some people stay stuck and continue repeating old, negative behaviors. Some people remain dangerous. I was lucky that I could see positive change happening in myself and those around me.

This is something you will need to discern for yourself. You can forgive people, let go of anger and still choose not to have them be part of your life.

The important thing is that you are no longer attached to the story. Forgiving is letting go of the story. As you grow and change, the story changes because how you view it changes. How you feel about it changes as you work through the emotions of it. You've experienced so much more since the story was written. You are no longer affected by it the same way. The people in the story hopefully change. It's like a sequel to a book. Threads of the story are the same but the circumstances and outcomes are different. It's time for a new book. And this is a tough one: you still need to work on understanding, accepting and possibly even loving that person. This is higher spiritual consciousness.

It might be easier to start with accepting the person as a fellow human being, then progressing to liking the parts of him or her that are likable. Again, this is a process, a journey, not a magic wand. Good people do bad things. You can love someone and not condone behavior. To be clear, forgiving is definitely not condoning behaviors as OK. You still hold people accountable. For example, if someone is toxic for me, just not good for me to be around, I can forgive the person *and* make sure at the same time he or she is not part of my life. I can understand why he or she might be behaving in a certain way and accept that for what it is in the moment. I can love that person as a human being and child of the Universe. Remember—every human on the planet is on a psycho-spiritual path of awakening. There are some ahead of you on the path and some behind you. Hating only eats away at you, does nothing to the other person and takes you farther away from Spirit. Practice non-judgment for those on the path behind you. Only love will bring them along. A challenge for sure!

I chose to look at the good, to *give first*. Forgiveness for me was made easier by knowing I could no longer be hurt. I had done my own inner work to be well. I was a thriving, healthy human being doing good things. Forgiveness was a journey, not an event. Real forgiveness occurred over time, not to be hurried. There was just no point in holding onto anger and hurt any more. What was done was done. Forgiveness was letting go of that anger, working it through and diffusing it. Then letting go a little bit more and a little bit more until there was nothing left to let go of, until it was all but extinguished, until the past no longer clouded my vision and I could see the person in the present. The past was no longer my story. I was living a new story, one in the present.

The present is the only thing that matters. When I stayed in the moment, in the present, guess what happened? I could love in that one singular moment. I could look at the person without the past whispering in my ear. It was only that one moment that counted, and in that moment all was well. A portal opened for more change to happen. The love rippled out into acceptance, and the people who hurt me received it. Again, *I* changed, not them. My change allowed an opening in my being, and they willingly ran through into my arms. Love poured down on me. Maybe forgiveness didn't have to come in words. It wasn't my journey to make sure someone understood, first, that there was wrongdoing and, second, that he or she needed to be forgiven. It was my journey to forgive. Forgiveness opens portals of love. Love heals all wounds. "Yes, you did this, and yes, I love you."

Long before I became aware, I used to think I was a male in my last lifetime who was rich and abused women. *Karma?* Not that I would ever choose to experience all that happened in my life, yet maybe I did choose this lifetime. Certainly, it gave me ample spiritual lessons and made me who I am today. *Chance?* I don't think so.

Wow, was I *grateful* for what happened in my life? I'm not sure I could say that then. I can say it now. I am grateful for my life and all its ups and downs, twists and turns. I wouldn't be writing this; I wouldn't be helping others become Soulfire Women if my life had been any different. I did realize there was a lot more to life than being hurt and angry. I started writing a gratitude journal, listing five things at the end of the day before bedtime I was grateful for, an idea made popular by Sarah Ban Breathnach in *Simple Abundance: A Daybook of Comfort and Joy*. Practicing gratitude was a game changer, a real shift in perception. Doing this simple thing turned any mood into a good mood and any day into a good day. Nothing really changed but my perception. Gratitude creates an energy field that's like a bullet train. When you incorporate gratitude into a wish, it's like putting it on the fast track to manifestation.

    I started practicing loving kindness, a Buddhist meditation and type of blessing for you as an infant, child, young adult; your loved ones; others with whom you are struggling; and the Earth as a whole. Joan Borysenko, Ph.D., in *Fire in the Soul*, offers the most beautiful loving kindness meditation. It shifted my perspective and my ability to love. It also helped me continue to heal my child and young adult self. And let me say this about Joan Borysenko, she was my best friend and mentor, although she doesn't know it, through most of my life. She started me on the psycho-spiritual path in *Guilt is the Teacher, Love is the Lesson,* followed by *Fire in the Soul.* Every book she wrote after that paralleled where I was in my life. You need to find an author or spiritual teacher like this to be your companion along the way.

    Love begins with you. I know it is cliché, but you have to love your perfectly imperfect self before you can move forward. Loving yourself happens when you forgive yourself. Forgive yourself first. Most women don't realize they are holding onto self-judgments—criticisms of things they did or didn't do; for not being perfect. They look back from an adult perspective and think they should have known better. This is an unfair judgment against yourself, looking back with today's eyes on the past. You cannot hold yourself accountable for what you didn't know. You did not have the wisdom then you have now. And what if you did know better? you argue. Well then, you were acting from an unhealed part of yourself. You were responding from a fragmented self, not your whole self. Let yourself off the hook.

Forgiving yourself is seismic. It is the self-love turning point, a moment of transition and transformation. Forgive yourself for not being perfect; for the list of things you did that you wish you hadn't done or those you wish you had done. You know what they are. List them, and with your hand over your heart, look in the mirror and say, *"I forgive you, (your name), from the deepest, most loving part of myself for_____. I understand I forgot who you were, your beauty, your true nature as a precious being. I love and honor all that you've been and all that you are. I love the whole of you, every part. I LOVE YOU."* Do this for every single perceived transgression on your list. Forgive yourself and you will feel the gateways to self-love open immediately.

Loving yourself is not about what you can do to make yourself better. Loving yourself is about taking away all of the things that made you forget you were perfect in the first place, all the layers of gunk. It's about being in love with you, an action, a feeling. Imagine you are a newborn baby, holding yourself for the first time, gazing into your own eyes. Can you feel that love? She is who you forgot. Find her. Bring her back. Be in love with *her*.

Soulfire Woman Principles

You have an unlimited capacity to love. Love is the vehicle of the Universe. It is fueled by forgiveness and joy.

Soulfire Women get angry. Not only is it allowed, it's encouraged. Fan the flame. It's where change happens and transformation takes place.

Take responsibility for yourself and your decisions, the good ones and not-so-good ones, without judgment. No blame game.

Step out and rise up out of victim consciousness. You are a strong and powerful woman!

Spiritual Lessons

God, Goddess, Spirit, Universal Energy, whatever you call it, is always with you and in you. You are never alone. Feel her. Cling to her like a life raft.

Life doesn't happen to you. It happens for you. Life gives you experiences and choices for your learning enjoyment.

Forgiveness and love start with forgiving and loving yourself first. Both are essential in your quest as a Soulfire Woman.

You always have free will in which the Universe intentionally does not interfere. It's part of your learning curve.

Psychological Truths

When the worst happens, you can and will survive. You may tank for a while; you can expect this. As you heal, your wisdom and resilience builds, and your ability to recover from difficult things increases. You build emotional strength. When you heal from your past wounds, you begin to see with clear vision how and why these events occurred. You know in a deep place you cannot be wounded this way again. Find strength and gratitude in this.

Hanging onto anger when you no longer need it only hurts you in the long run. You risk becoming bitter and ill. The truth is: no one cares about your anger except you. You deserve peace.

Anger is a secondary feeling. There is always a primary feeling there first before you feel the anger. It's fleeting; you need to catch it. It's the underneath feeling that holds the charge. For example, often underneath anger is fear or hurt. This is where the work needs to happen.

You can very often *choose* your feelings just as you can change your thoughts. When your thoughts change, your feelings change. I can call myself stupid or instead say, "I learned from that and will make a different decision next time." Feel the difference?

You must work on healing yourself first before you can truly forgive others. When you heal yourself, you become aware of your actions and react less out of hurt and more from authenticity and love. It is from this real place that forgiveness happens.

Setting Your Soul on Fire

Start a gratitude journal. List five things every day before you go to bed for which you are grateful. You don't have to be profound here. You can be grateful the sun came up, the promise of a new day. Every day is a new beginning. *The Gratitude Connection: Embrace the Positive Power of Thanks* by Amy Collette is a great book to help you with this.

Loving yourself is not just an affirmation. You don't just look in the mirror and say, "I love you." Well, you can, it does help. I mean the kind of loving yourself that is from the inside out. You fall in love with yourself. It means you love all your selves, your imperfections and quirks. The Universe conspired to make a unique you. There's no one on this planet just like you. You are divinely inspired with Divine purpose.

Start by sitting quietly, close your eyes, slowing and deepening your breath. Drop your awareness from your head into your heart. Breathe in and out of your heart center. Now recall a time when you felt deeply loved. This may be by a beloved person or a pet, from the eyes of a child or maybe when you extended an act of kindness—a time when love washed over you and through you. Feel it. Really feel it. Now hold onto this feeling, breathing it into your whole body. Feel it pulsate. Let it envelope you.

Make a list of 100 things you really like about yourself. I know it sounds scary. Don't worry. You're going to be surprised at how much you really do like. Number your paper from 1-100 and write as quickly as you can. Don't worry, you can repeat yourself when you feel stuck. At some point you will move from your conscious to your subconscious self where delightful surprises await you.

Write yourself a love letter. Really. Be mushy, gushy and super kind. Use your list of 100 to help you. Then mail it to yourself. Or give it to a friend to mail to you at some random time. Or hide it somewhere you will find it much later. You will feel amazing when you receive it! You can also write yourself a letter of thanksgiving or gratitude and mail it.

Practice loving kindness meditations.

Feeling angry or depressed means that something in your life needs to change. It's an opportunity to take a deeper look at what's causing the anger or depression. Everyone's choices are the same: You can do nothing. You can change your behavior and how you react. You can change how you think about it; your perspective. Or, you can change your situation.

How you think about something determines how you feel about it. For example, if I tell myself it's all my fault my relationship did not work out, then I feel like a failure and awful about myself. If I tell myself there are two people in every relationship, and both are at fault, then I can own what's mine, learn from, it and leave the rest. I feel like I have some sense of control. While I may feel upset or disappointed, I am not blaming myself.

The answers to your blocks to change are in your resistance. Whenever you feel resistant toward something, that's where you dig deeper to find the real cause.

Identify and know your triggers—when your buttons are being pushed. Be aware, stop, press pause and make a conscious choice as to how you are going to respond. If you can't do this, begin by journaling about your triggers: What makes me react the way I do? How did the triggers start? Is it certain people, places or things? Gaining mastery over your emotional responses will help you feel more in control; like you are on solid ground.

Begin a path of forgiveness, starting with yourself. When you hold judgment against yourself, you separate yourself from Divine love. Forgive yourself like you are forgiving your best friend, a person you would never ever want to be without or hold a grudge against. Write yourself a letter of forgiveness. Write another letter from a more loving part of yourself.

Once you feel like you have reasonably accomplished this first step in forgiveness, then begin to forgive others in your life. Start by writing from another's perspective. This will take you out of your narrow view and help you understand better how the other person is feeling.

Go back to your genogram and use this as a map of understanding your family ties. It will give you clearer vision. Understanding gives you perspective—it's for you, not the other person. When you understand something, see it in context because it enables you to let go. It does not mean you let people off the hook for their behaviors. You let yourself off the hook. Patterns are coded in our heredity and have a strong force field. It takes a strong person to break the chain. You are doing it—breaking the genetic link in that chain link fence. You are a Soulfire Woman!

Practice loving unconditionally, loving without attachment to behaviors. This can be hard. Start with a pet. Volunteer. It might help to start with people you don't know, for whom you have no expectations. Expectations always get you into trouble because they set up conditions. Live without expectations, with awareness in every moment. Anchor yourself in the present moment.

Compassion will be an outgrowth of loving unconditionally. Remember—compassion doesn't mean pity. It is an act of love.

Freedom: Stepping Into Soulfire Woman Power

Feelings are the language of the Soul moving into the deepest parts of yourself where transformation happens. Feelings and transformation go hand and hand. Sacred Alchemy.

FREEDOM IN MY STORY DID NOT BEGIN as you might think. I was about to celebrate my 25th wedding anniversary. My daughter headed off to college. I started my own business, giving me the freedom to finally travel with my husband, who had been around the world and back while I tended the home fires and kept a job. I was soooo looking forward to this next phase in our lives.

But then... Whoa! Hold up a minute! I began noticing old familiar patterns of behavior from him, although I was not quite sure at first. My father-in-law developed lung cancer and was given a short time to live. The family, all of us, took it very hard, especially my husband. He also had a hard time when our daughter went off to college, despite him being away from home a good bit of the time. He seemed depressed, I thought. He would come home at the end of the week and fall asleep in the chair. We were operating on different waves of energy. I couldn't wait for him to come home so we could reconnect and enjoy each other's company. He, on the other hand, came home and crashed and stayed that way until he left again for work on Monday.

Hitting Your Stride, Finding Your Identity

I talked with him about it. I was using my voice, not reading his mind. It was our problem, not my problem to fix. I encouraged him to see a doctor for depression. He didn't. It only got worse. There were other behaviors that made me start to feel suspicious, such as not being available at certain times, being edgy and short with me, not wanting to do anything together, and most apparent, changes in the bedroom. A woman knows these things. It was time to get my head out of the sand. Again. For whatever reason, his business bills were addressed to both of us. While I had never paid attention before, I thought, Why not take a look? Sure enough, he wasn't where he had said he was. There were purchases for flowers, clothes, hotels, dinners. Here we go again, I thought. This time I wasted no time in confronting him with what I had found. I was not graceful. I was in Warrior Goddess mode. Of course, he tried to deflect by blaming me for opening the bill despite my name being on the front of the envelope. Then the implausible explanation came. The difference? I didn't doubt myself this time. I didn't accept the explanations. And most importantly, I didn't blame myself. I held strong. I kept my power. I knew I was not to blame for whatever behaviors he used to cope with whatever he was dealing with at the time. I knew who I was unequivocally. And that was that. He took his ring off, put it on the counter, said he was unhappy, that he couldn't be married any longer, and walked out for good.

Let's be clear here. I had started to suspect for a long while after I began to realize depression was not the whole of it and before I took the step to finally know the truth. I suspect I did know the truth and was preparing myself for the inevitable. I was getting ready for the storm, gathering my own strength. Confrontation does not have to be immediate. It can happen when you are ready and on your own terms. When you are aware, you get to choose your moments instead of your moments choosing you.

Even though I knew the truth, I still wailed and wailed. I was grieving the loss as it was happening, a necessary step to moving forward. There was no fighting back this time. It was over. Although in reality I know I got up for work every day, continuing with my routine, it felt like I sat on the deck and didn't move for a year. I knew my husband would never file for divorce, and it would have to be me to initiate the process. Again, I needed the strength first. I stayed put, rocked myself soothingly on that deck like I remembered my grandmother rocking me, started reading the *Outlander* series by Diana Gabaldon, whose characters became my friends, and healed. I drew strength from Claire, a strong, independent, intelligent, powerful woman who overcomes obstacle after obstacle. I was in total awareness. This is the difference. Even when I didn't agree with my own behaviors and choices, I was still in total awareness, choosing them anyway and letting that be OK. I allowed the feelings to come, to just be. I was deep in pain and grief, crying so hard I could barely breathe at times. To keep myself from going over the edge emotionally, I would look across the fields and notice how vivid the varied colors of green were in the trees. I watched them sway like a slow dance yet stay rooted. If I stayed here, *present*, not in the past or the future, if I was *mindful* of my surroundings, I could be all right. I merged with the Earth and grounded myself there. Nature was my solace. I had full knowledge that I could survive this despite the sense of loss and despair I felt. I didn't have to emotionally manipulate the situation out of fear of abandonment. Spirit would never abandon me, I knew. I was physically abandoned, and I could still be OK, of this I was sure.

I let the tears roll, and they did. Wherever I was—when I was working out at the Y, shopping at the grocery store, watching TV, reading a book, driving to a friend's, lying awake at night in bed. I let them come, knowing they were a cleansing gift from God(dess). And I was still *grateful*. In spite of my very human response, I could still see the big picture. I was grateful that my husband's unhappiness and behaviors forced me to look at myself and see, try as I might, that I could not control anything or anyone in order to make myself feel more secure. It made me take the path of healing myself. I was grateful for the good years we had. Those years gave me time to grow. We just eventually grew apart. In his defense, he would say we never should have gotten married in the first place, that he was unhappy a long time. A logical person would agree with him. The signs were there from day one. I "should" have known better. All I really knew at the time was dysfunction, and our relationship felt right that way. I didn't know I had grown so used to dysfunction it seemed normal. What I do know is this: we had a Divine contract to fulfill. If we had not married, we would not have brought our gifted daughter into this world, who is on her own journey of higher consciousness. I would not have been united with my family. We partnered to expose our pasts, bring them into the present and complete them. I suppose I can only speak for myself here. Without this partnership I may have been stuck for another lifetime. The problems in our marriage forced me to look deeper into my past where the real issues were. Otherwise, I might have lived out my days harboring a crippling secret. Our union was destiny from the beginning. I felt the joy of family and tradition. There was just so much good, it would be hard not to be grateful.

One day I got up from the deck and filed for divorce.

I could feel grateful and still step into my fiery Warrior Goddess when it came time to hire lawyers. The divorce did not end amicably as I had hoped. Here's the thing about feelings; you rarely feel one way or the other. There are usually a whole host of mixed-up feelings in there, some in juxtaposition with each other, like loving and loathing at the same time. You are not your thoughts nor are you your feelings. Thank goodness. Feelings are feelings. They are not fact. They are conduits of information. Feelings carry the waves of emotion needed for healing. Feelings are the language of your soul, moving into the deepest parts of yourself where transformation happens. Feelings and transformation go hand and hand. Sacred Alchemy.

So what part of this is freeing? The part where I navigated with complete awareness. It did not spare me grief or misfortune. It helped me know the truth of the situation and navigate it with as little anger and bitterness as I could.

Freedom is not being tied to invisible strings. You see with complete clarity. Your inner space is clear. When you are clear, your intuition (God, Goddess, Spirit) guides you more than hurt, anger and fear do.

There is freedom in also remembering who you are without this person. Who am I? I asked myself again. Who am I without having to accommodate another? This time I was not so scared of the answer—I knew I was in there somewhere—I knew I was somebody. She was there patiently waiting to be rediscovered. Along the way I found my identity, my authentic self. I stopped trying to be perfect and felt complete as perfectly imperfect. I felt more than good enough. I used my voice.

And most importantly, I kept my *power*.

Women Need Women to Heal

I had really wanted to attend a Modern Day Priestess training through the Institute of Modern Wisdom with the Rev. Dr. Kate Rodger. I hadn't signed up for a number of reasons related to cost and time away. *I'm going* was my first independent decision and barely three weeks after my husband left his ring on the counter. I made last-minute flight arrangements and got on the plane. Luckily, another attendee met me at the LA airport and drove us the rest of the way to Santa Barbara. I told her my story. She quietly listened.

In a room with two other women, I could barely speak I was so raw. As soon as they left the room, I stood there choking on my tears. I called my friend, stammering that I didn't know why I came, I was barely functional. She said very calmly, "There must be a reason why you are there. You are there, try to make the best of it." I couldn't muster the energy to connect with the other women. I could speak my rawness with vulnerability and openness in our circles though. It resonated. I felt the love. They let me *be*. I could feel the power of the feminine collective. The circle held me. Women need women to heal. It was here I learned that you are not your story. I learned how everything is energy and how language affects energy and outcome. "But" negates, and "try" means you are not committed. "I don't know" is not an answer. You always know. Always. Excuses are just that. Excuses. If you want to do something, you will find a way. We left with prayer and Soul Remembering partners to connect with weekly by phone. I learned to pray in a positive, affirmative way using spiritual principles and laws. Soul Remembering took me to the depths of my soul and transmuted and healed those raw feelings. I am forever in debt to my partners, who elevated my soul, kept me afloat and saved me from sinking. I learned how to say yes to life.

It was not possible to stay in our family home and move on with my life. I was too attached to all of the memories there as well as to my soon-to-be ex-husband's family. I knew their allegiance would always be to him, although if I chose to, I could remain a part of the family. In my heart I knew it would keep me stagnant, unable to heal and recover, and would inevitably create more pain. I made the hard choice of separating myself over time. I experienced another deeper layer of letting go of attachments: the physical attachment to that home, hearth and family as it was; the intangible attachment to our future lives together, reaping the rewards of all those years of hard work; and the hardest of all, leaving my daughter to sort it out for herself. Layer after layer of attachment came peeling away. I was raw and open. *I* was all that was left.

Caught again in the spiral of healing, I went backwards and forwards, up and down. I recognized the healing path this time. I moved back into my first chakra and decided I needed to get a stable job with benefits. I needed security. I also needed to feel like I could stand on my own two feet. My spiritual work was done there, I truly felt that, and I needed to grow into a new place. It was the long goodbye. The long, painful goodbye for my soul's growth.

In looking back, I can also see my moving was for the soul growth of all those connected to me: my daughter, my closest friends and my family. Everyone shifted in her own way, dug deeper into her own soul. Most came out richer, more complete. It felt like a Divine sacrifice, albeit painful, for the good of all. I can also see that my own soul growth in this relationship had ended a long time ago. While I could say I moved where I found a job, four states away, I really moved where I felt drawn, where my intuition told me I would find love. I moved in service of love. I listened to *her*—my Soulfire Woman.

Soulfire Woman Principles

True freedom is when you step into your full Soulfire Woman Power. Soulfire Power is knowing your true identity, remembering who you really are, your core essence. It's making decisions from this place of knowing, free and clear of emotional blocks and the unconscious past. It's hanging onto the strength of who you are, knowing you and the Sacred Feminine, the Divine, are One.

See with clarity, however painful. Truth always. Awareness always. Hiding from the truth clouds your vision, keeps you stuck in your patterns and limits your choices.

Warrior Goddesses prepare for battle, build strength and gather resources. Circle the wagons, ladies. Gather the women who will support, love and teach you.

Get on your pedestal. Rise above the fray. Spread those wings. Soulfire Women make decisions from the perspective of strength, gratitude and love. Soulfire Women do not make knee-jerk reactions to emotions or inflict pain or take revenge.

You always know the answer. Always. It is within at all times.

As Earth Mothers, we love and protect the Earth!

Spiritual Lessons

You enter into Divine contracts with others throughout your life. There is always a reason. Contracts in this lifetime sometimes come to an end, which means a soul expansion is ahead of you.

When you are aware, you make choices with clarity. Even when you make not-so-good choices, you are still doing them with open eyes. Being aware does not mean you choose perfectly.

When you learn to stay in the moment, to be mindful, you fine-tune your gratitude skills.

Feelings and transformation go hand and hand. Sacred Alchemy.

Clarity and truth are the path of wisdom.

Psychological Truths

If you let go of expectations, you will heal faster.

If you let go of attachments, you will heal on the deepest level.

When you are aware, you get to choose your moments instead of your moments choosing you.

You are not your feelings. Your feelings are not necessarily fact. They are guideposts to your truth and healing.

You have to set an intention and *feel* it before it will come into being. If your subconscious is sabotaging you, for example saying you are unworthy of a relationship, your intention will not come into being or you will attract someone who validates your unconscious beliefs. Invisible energies are the covert ways you stay stuck by denying, projecting, emotionally manipulating, disconnecting and _____ (add your own here).

Setting Your Soul on Fire

You are now fine-tuning becoming a Soulfire Woman. Practice and enhance what you already know. Navigate life with complete awareness.

Practice mindfulness and staying present. Be in the moment. In this moment, right now, you are fine. Breathe. Literally live moment to moment. When your mind wanders, take yourself back to this moment. Notice how the air feels on your skin, the sun on your face, the colors that surround you, the smell of the place. This is reality, not your thoughts or worries.

Journal about:

> Who am I really, without this person or situation in my life?
>
> How have I compromised myself, my soul?
>
> Where do I need to make changes?

Do a cluster journal exercise on Soulfire Divine Feminine Power. Clustering is like brainstorming using free association. It's done quickly in two to three minutes. Place the words "Soulfire Divine Feminine Power" in the middle of your page, circle it and then free associate from there. Whatever pops into your head, draw a line from the center circle, write it down, circle it and keep going. What pops into your mind next? Does it come off of the main circle or the one you just wrote? Keep going. Move quickly. Once you start thinking, stop. You are done. You will know immediately where to find your power. It's essential knowledge.

Fine-tune your identity. Look to the past. What were you like as a child? What did you enjoy most? What were your favorite pastimes, favorite games? What made you happy? What joyful memories come to mind when you close your eyes? Maybe take the time to collage this or write about it in your journal. Now, how congruent is your current life with your childhood fantasies and desires? You are moving toward authenticity.

Is there someplace in your life you're acting, literally acting, a place not authentically you? For example, some women do not let on how smart they really are to assuage the egos around them. Get to the why of this; why are you acting? Who would you be if you didn't pretend? Are you soothing your own fears or someone else's?

List 10 people you really admire. List what you really like about them. This is your guide to who you really are or want to be. Do this first before you read the next sentence.

The qualities you list are ones you really have or ones you aspire to. Make it happen.

Are you using your voice? Being assertive, kind and direct? Where can you speak your truth more often?

Leave "shoulds" at the door. They only serve to make you feel guilty and keep you stuck in the past. Replace any "shoulds" with "coulds," a more accurate assessment of any situation. You will immediately feel the difference in your body. It's almost like it breathes a sigh of relief, a big exhale.

Honor your feelings. They will pass like a slow-motion wave. Stay with them until they transform into action or movement. If you feel stuck in your feelings, look at your thoughts. Are you choosing to think about something in such a way that makes you feel the way you do? Is there another way to look at the situation, a change of perspective that will shift how you feel?

Are there any residual, covert beliefs you are holding onto that may be keeping you stuck? For example, "Good girls don't get angry; crying makes you weak..." These are rules programmed during our childhoods, often before the age of 7, that are just not true and only serve to bind you and keep you from stepping into your full Soulfire Woman self. Subconscious beliefs create patterns and condition your responses to life.

Clear your chakras daily, using sound, vibration, visualization or dance. A simple way is taking a rainbow shower. Imagine each of the colors of the chakras as the water washes through you, clearing away any debris.

Laugh a lot. Laughter is instant healing. The vibration shakes your core and knocks stuff loose. It just disappears into the ether. Dance it off. Sing. These are all ways to change your vibration.

Live a Higher-Consciousness Life On Purpose

Loving me makes loving everyone else extra special, like a gift from Spirit, a beautifully wrapped present I get to open up every day.

I HAD THREE WEEKS TO PACK UP a household of 25 years and move. This was not a lot of time, yet if I'd had any more I might have changed my mind. Each friend showed up in turn to help me sort through my things: keep and retrieve later, give away, throw away, take with me. I was downsizing, moving into a condo overlooking a small lake. My best friend and her husband arrived to drive me the distance, he in the U-Haul and each of us with a packed-to-the-gills car. Pulling out that morning with my daughter standing in the driveway was the hardest thing I've ever done. It should have been the other way around, she off living her life somewhere and me waiting for her visits home. Although an adult, she was still finding her way, and was also dealing with her parents' divorce. My friends, who were supposed to stay the weekend at my new place, informed me they had to leave the next day. I felt like my parents had just dropped me off at college for the first time. All I could do was cry. Thankfully, my friend insisted I get my kitchen together before she left, a godsend since cooking is healing and soothing to me. Having no one to cook for was one of the ways I felt my losses the deepest.

New home. New beginning. Now what? I went back to work as a college counselor, something I knew I did well and could do without a learning curve. I did not anticipate that I was taking a job at a counseling center just finding its way and lacking in many respects, primarily staff. I thought I would quickly hit my stride offering mind/body, journaling and yoga wellness groups, as I had done at my previous position years before. My current boss told me she had never heard of the word "chakras." She was the anxious type and worried I might touch someone. Literally. Not a good sign. We were severely understaffed. The stress overcame me. I was having trouble sticking to my routine of meditation and journaling, my grounding forces. I could, though, stay connected and present with nature and focused on the ducks in the pond and my beloved dog. I could barely handle my caseload let alone offer anything additional.

The center reflected the town, behind the times with small pockets of spiritually minded people. Just where had I landed? I thought I would pick up exactly where I had left off in Pennsylvania with a private practice offering energy healing, journal groups and so on. Not to be. Now I had all the skills I needed to live a higher-consciousness life on purpose, I *knew* what to do, yet felt like I had hit a brick wall.

I was able to find a group of Laconneau women practicing a Gnostic tradition dating back thousands of years to Mary Magdalene. I found a home, a light in the dark. Laconneau is practical living on the way to enlightenment. I read *The Gospel of the Beloved Companion*, the original Gospel of Mary Magdalene, translated by Jehanne de Quillan. This Gospel is a complete guide to higher consciousness, moving you through the boughs of a tree—eight limbs to enlightenment. In my own way I had been practicing this all along. I was here on purpose to find these teachings and to experience higher consciousness in the flesh. At gatherings I was able to see and witness, on occasion, beyond my eyes into other dimensions, confirmation of all that is possible without self-imposed limitations. An example of the teaching is to pause before responding and ask yourself, "Is it kind, is it necessary, is it relevant?"

Everyone is on the path, some behind you, some ahead of you. Darkness is the absence of light. Do the work. Do the work. Do the work. Decisions are made by consensus. No gossiping. Deal with issues directly, kindly and with love. Forgive means *giving first*. You and the Divine Mother are one and the same. And, the Divine Mother has a sense of humor.

BEing Spiritually Resilient

Then I got a new boss. The devil stepped in and took me through hell. I remembered saying to myself after my separation that I wanted to personally work on responding from a place of *wisdom* and not from my emotions. My emotions overtook me easily in the days after the divorce: the move, the new job, being away from friends and family. Wait. Did Spirit hear me ask for this lesson?

I was in full awareness of two things: I needed to practice coming from a place of love and to respond with wisdom. We are on higher-level learning, walk the talk, I said to myself. This person was hard for me to love. I reflected the light on his darkness. I worked and worked at being the Light. Address the behavior, not the person, I reminded myself. Everyone is on the path, I repeated. Some are behind me and some are ahead of me. I was aware every single time I resorted to my old ways. I did not judge myself when I didn't get it right. Every day was a new day, a new way to try again. I was in soul training. I also had choices. I could have easily left this position, yet I stayed. I knew I was doing soul work. In time, others on the staff would respond and move with the Light, of this I was sure. I could either lower my vibration to the level of the office, gossiping, dividing allegiances (which I did at times, knowingly), or I could raise the office to a higher vibration. This is when you press pause and weigh your responses and actions. There were times I broke down from the stress of it all. My first chakra would take hold of me and whisper, *Security, security, security* in my ear. If I had left the position then, nothing would have been accomplished. No movement for me or anyone else. I needed to stay until I completed my spiritual lessons. It was my choice. I practiced non-attachment. I got better and better at it. It was time to surrender, to stop trying so hard, to be still and listen. And then one fateful Friday, he was let go. The darkness lifted and the light poured in. You could really feel it moving through the halls like a golden river. Smiles came out with the sunshine. The energy of the place lifted. Truth, the *Light* always wins.

In Service of Something Greater Than Yourself—Love

In the midst of all of this, I found love. I wrote down all of the things I wanted in a partner. I was specific about it, including a full head of hair. I decided I didn't want to date. I was never very good at it anyway. My plan was to meet the right person from the start; I would know him as soon as I met him. I held out for nearly a year after my arrival, tried to force Divine timing, and decided I would have to resort to the dating sites. Meanwhile my landlady kept telling me, "Just wait, just wait, I have someone for you."

I went ahead and tried to sign up on three different sites on three separate occasions. Each time, for whatever reason (ha! we know the reason), it did not work. Then my landlady called me and asked if I wanted to go with her to see a band at the local country club. Of course!

She wanted to know what I was wearing and approved. Odd, I thought at the time. Off we went, and she introduced me to this guy who worked next to her office. I thought I was a cover for the two of them to get together. He was cute and from the Northeast. We had a lot in common. Someone suggested we dance. "Next date," he said.

It hit me—this was a set-up. I was actually on a blind date! *Nice.*

Divine timing. Things happen at just the right time, which is not necessarily your time. Put the intention out there, trust and wait. When it does happen, you realize instantly why it happened in just that moment.

Finding myself in a new relationship after a quarter century with one man is exciting, new, and to say the least, challenging. How to keep your spiritual center, your authentic self while being partnered is a true test of spiritual awakening. That story may be another book for another time.

Our relationship continues, and as all relationships do, has its ups and downs and challenges. My biggest challenge is not to lose myself, my own identity in someone else and not to fall so easily into my caretaker role. I'm doing a good job this time around. I work hard at not silencing myself out of habit. Instead of being the relationship peacemaker, always letting my needs be secondary, I use my voice with clarity and strength. I choose me, unequivocally, SoulFULLY and without apology as the first love of my life. Loving me makes loving everyone else extra special, like a gift from Spirit, a beautifully wrapped present I get to open up every day.

I continue to learn my spiritual lessons and still sometimes get hit over the head with spiritual two-by-fours. Reminding myself not to push so hard, to be in an open state of grace, allowing Spirit to co-create with me is a daily check-in with my heart, body, mind and soul. Most importantly I remember who I am. I reclaim her every day and reignite the Soulfire Woman Power within me. I am whole, mostly healed, all the parts of me now residing in one dwelling—my scared child, my imperfect self and especially my most powerful authentic Soulfire Woman self. It feels like coming full circle, born as love and returning to love consciousness as the force that fuels the Universe and my whole being.

My awakening hasn't stopped. I continue weaving my tapestry, adding threads of healing and spiritual revelations as I move through midlife and beyond. My forgiveness is deeper and my love stronger. I *choose* who to be. My story is your story. And in the end the story never really mattered. It was the *energy* of the story, the feelings attached to it that needed to be healed and transformed. My story doesn't define me or hold me captive because there is no longer any energy attached to it. Living and being in the present is a saving grace that way. There's no past dragging me down. In this moment, right now, breath to breath, all is good. Not that I don't get triggered once in a while. I do. When that happens, I recognize it as best I can and work through it in the ways I've opened up to you about in this book. My hope in sharing my journey with you is that you are able to see yourself, use what I know to be true, heal right along with me and step into your own power. I wish for you to be who you were always meant to be, a Soulfire Woman.

And so it is.

Soulfire Woman Principles

Soulfire Women do not gossip. We deal directly with kindness and love.

Soulfire Women operate using the four C's:

    Collaboration
    Cohesion
    Consensus
    Courage

Spiritual Lessons

We are One. You know this now. Your Divine Essence, the spark that lives within you and lights your entire being, is connected to every other living thing. How can we not be One when we share breath with the entire planet!

There is an untouchable part of you always connected to Spirit. You are never, ever alone.

There is Divine timing. If you and the Divine are One, it would make sense that timing is really collaborative, agreed upon in the unseen or before time itself, yes? Even if you can't wrap your head around it, trust it as truth.

Joy and bliss are a by-product of love and vice versa.

Divine service. What gifts do you have that you can give in service of divine love?

Psychological Truths

When your values, ethics, thoughts and behaviors match, inside and out, you are living an authentic life. You are the same person wherever you are, with no facades. You are living your truth.

Lasting change is created from within. Spiritual resilience *is* psychological resilience and well-being. You cannot separate the two.

Setting Your Soul on Fire

You are now living as a Soulfire Woman. No more excuses. Ever. You have clear vision.

The responsibility for your life lies with you. Use your intuition and soul guidance unencumbered by old patterns and past hurts to guide you. *This is freedom.*

Meditation, journaling, chakra cleansing, energy healing, body scans, nutrition, prayer, yoga, sounding, singing, dancing, nature, reading, friends and so on, sustain you on every level. It is the food of the mind, body and soul. Not all at once of course. Develop and pick a combination of what works for you to keep yourself free of emotional blocks, to remain psychologically and physically open and clear. It's the key to your freedom.

You are now so in tune with yourself that you immediately notice any subtle change in your thoughts, feelings, energy or body and know your attention is being called there to shift, transmute or transform. You follow your intuition and Spirit without hesitation.

Congratulations! You have arrived, Soulfire Woman!

Soulfire Woman: How to Torch Your Past, Ignite Your Present and Set Your Soul on Fire

Answer the primal call to your own **authenticity**

Be in your **truth** always;

Feel and **heal** the past;

Connect mind, body and Soulfire for **intuitive wisdom**;

Forgive yourself first and **self-love** follows;

Find your **voice**;

Step into your true **identity**;

Free your **Soulfire Divine Feminine Power**

And this is it, how to live a higher-consciousness life on purpose. Your life is going to unfold as it unfolds. As it does, you develop spiritual muscle and resilience by following the Soulfire Woman's Way. It's like the yellow brick road back to *you*. You do not have to be fixed. You have to be found. Your Soulfire Power is in knowing there is an untouchable part of yourself—your soul—who is always connected to Spirit, your life source, like an umbilical cord. She is there, always. Dance with her. Sing her Divine glory. Peel away the stories, the layers of guilt and shame. They are not you. Over time it will take you less and less time to move through the healing process. You'll be able to achieve this in an instant with Spirit flowing through you as one consciousness. You will never see anything the same way again.

With gratitude, humility and love, Dyanne

Come see me at soulfirewoman.com. We'll walk the Soulfire Woman's Way together!

Book Club Questions

1. The author states that her story is not really that important, yet tells it to the reader as a universal story for women. What stories do women as a group tell themselves? How do these stories hold women back from being authentic, being who they really are and want to be? Can stories be rewritten?
2. How do you define power? Where do women gain or lose power personally, in relationships, work and/or families? How is personal power restored once lost? What makes you feel most powerful?
3. Where do women draw their strength and emotional resiliency from in life?
4. How can women maintain their own identities and at the same time fulfill their many roles in life? Do you believe there is a difference between SoulFULL and SelfLESS?
5. Do you believe, as the author states, that you can only change yourself? How does this work in friendships, partnerships and parenting?
6. Do you think women's voices are silenced? How? How do you silence yourself? Why?
7. The author states that things don't happen to you, they happen for you. In your reflections on personal experiences, can you see how an event created a turning point of personal growth for you in life?
8. Feelings are often avoided as being unpleasant or unimportant. How do you *feel* about the idea of needing to feel to heal? Have you ever experienced how a release of feelings has helped you move past something painful?

9. How do you feel Spirit in your life? Do you feel connected to something beyond yourself? Do you feel your mind, body, soul and Spirit as intertwined and working together on your behalf and for your best self?
10. Women often disconnect from their bodies, judging them as imperfect in many ways. Would how you view your body change if you knew your body was a valuable conduit of intuitive information? How do you connect with your body?
11. How important do you think self-love is to your sense of well-being and ability to love others in turn? Is self-love easy or difficult for you? How about self-forgiveness?
12. Do you notice synchronicities in your life? What are they? Do you view them as meaningful coincidences giving you direction?
13. Do you believe in the idea that you have to remember who you are rather than be fixed?

Resources

Visit http://soulfirewoman.com/resources for a complete list of Dyanne's favorite resources.

Kathleen Adams, M.A.—*Journal to the Self: 22 Paths to Personal Growth*

Joan Anderson—*A Year by the Sea: Thoughts of an Unfinished Woman*

Ellen Bass and Laura Davis—*The Courage to Heal: A Guide for Women Survivors of Child Sexual Abuse*

Melody Beattie—*Codependent No More: How to Stop Controlling Others and Start Caring for Yourself*

Jean Shinoda Bolen, M.D.—*Crossing Avalon: A Woman's Midlife Quest for the Scared Feminine*

Joan Borysenko, Ph.D.:
- *7 Paths to God: The Ways of the Mystic*
- *A Woman's Book of Life: The Biology, Psychology, and Spirituality of the Feminine Life Cycle*
- *A Woman's Journey to God*
- *Fire in the Soul*
- *Guilt is the Teacher, Love is the Lesson: A Book to Heal You, Heart and Soul*
- *Minding the Body, Mending the Mind*
- *Pocketful of Miracles: Prayers, Meditation, and Affirmations to Nurture Your Spirit Every Day of the Year*

Tara Brach, Ph. D.—*Radical Acceptance: Embracing Your Life with the Heart of a Buddha*

Marion Zimmer Bradley—*Mists of Avalon*

Sara Ban Breathnach—*Simple Abundance: A Daybook of Comfort of Joy*

Kathleen A. Brehony—*Awakening at Midlife: A Guide to Reviving Your Spirit, Recreating Your Life and Returning to Your Truest Self*

Joseph Campbell with Bill Moyers—*The Power of Myth*

Doc Childre and Howard Martin with Donna Beech—*The Heartmath Solution*

Paulo Coehlo—*The Alchemist*

Amy Collette—*The Gratitude Connection: Embrace the Positive Power of Thanks*

Jehanne DeQuillan (translation and commentary)—*The Gospel of the Beloved Companion: The Complete Gospel of Mary Magdalene*

Louise DeSalvo, Ph. D.—*Writing as a Way of Healing*

Donna Eden with David Feinstein—*Energy Medicine*

Debbie Ford:
- *The Dark side of Light Chasers*
- *Spiritual Divorce*

Shakti Gawain:
- *Creative Visualization*
- *Developing Intuition: Practical Guidance for Daily Life*
- *The Four Levels of Healing: A Guide to Balancing the Spiritual, Mental, Emotional, and Physical Aspects of Life*

Elizabeth Gilbert—*Eat Pray Love: One Woman's Search for Everything Across Italy, India and Indonesia*

Natalie Goldberg—*Writing Down the Bones: Freeing the Writer Within*

Joel S. Goldsmith—*Practicing the Presence*

Louise Hay—*You Can Heal Your Life*

Kate Horsley—*Confessions of a Pagan Nun: A Novel*

H.B. Jeffery—*The Principles of Healing*

Otto Kroeger and Janet M. Thuesen—*Type Talk: The 16 Personality Types that Determine How We live, Love, and Work*

Joseph and Lilian Le Page—*Mudras: For Healing and Transformation*

Elizabeth Lesser—*Broken Open: How Difficult Times Can Help Us Grow*

Denise Linn—*Soul Couching: 28 Days to Discover Your Authentic Self*

Monica McGoldrick, Randy Gerson—*Genograms in Family Assessment*

Lewis Mehl-Madrona, M.D. *Coyote Medicine*

Sue Monk Kidd—*The Dance of the Dissident Daughter*

Thomas Moore—*Care of the Soul: A Guide for Cultivating Depth and Sacredness in Everyday Life*

Bill Moyers—*Healing and the Mind*

Caroline Myss:
- *Anatomy of the Spirit: The Seven Stages of Power and Healing*
- *Energy Anatomy: The Science of Personal Power, Spirituality, and Health*

Belleruth Naparstek—*Staying Well with Guided Imagery: How to Harness the Power of Your Imagination for Health and Healing*

Nancy J. Napier:
- *Getting Through the Day: Strategies for Adults Hurt as Children*
- *Recreating Your Life: Help for Adult Children of Dysfunctional Families*

Carol Emery Normandi and Laurelee Roark—*It's Not About Food: Change Your Mind, Change Your Life, End Your Obsession with Food and Weight*

Christiane Northrup, M.D.—*Women's Bodies, Women's Wisdom: Creating Physical and Emotional Health and Healing*

Elaine Pagels—*The Gnostic Gospels*

Dr. Eric Pearl—*The Reconnection*

Candace B. Pert, Ph.D.—*Everything You Need to Know to Feel Go(o)d*

Ira Progroff—*At a Journal Workshop: The basic text and guide for using the Intensive Journal Process*

James Redfield—*The Celestine Prophecy: An Adventure*

Cheryl Richardson—*The Unmistakable Touch of Grace*

Lynn A. Robinson—*Trust Your Gut: How the Power of Intuition Can Grow Your Business*

Geneen Roth—*When Food is Love: Exploring the Relationship Between Eating and Intimacy*

Ron Roth, Ph.D. with Peter Occhiogrossso:
- *Holy Spirit for Healing: Merging Ancient Wisdom with Modern Medicine*
- *Prayer and the Five Stages of Healing*
- *Reclaim Your Spiritual Power*
- *The Healing Path of Prayer: A Modern Mystic's Guide to Spiritual Power*

Don Miguel Ruiz—*The Four Agreements*

Jamie Sams and David Carson—*Medicine Cards*

Helen Schucman—*A Course in Miracles: Foundation for Inner Peace*

Cheryl Strayed—*Wild*

Lynda Terry—*The 11 Intentions: Invoking the Sacred Feminine as a Pathway to Inner Peace*

Colin Tipping—*Radical Forgiveness*

Eckhart Tolle—*The Power of Now*

Anodea Judith and Selene Vega—*The Sevenfold Journey: Reclaiming Mind, Body & Spirit Through the Chakras*

Doreen Virtue, Ph.D.—*Healing with the Angels: How the Angels Can Assist You in Every Area of Your Life*

Amy Weintraub—*Yoga for Depression: A Compassionate Guide to Relieve Suffering Through Yoga*

Tara Westover—*Educated: A Memoir*

Charles L. Whitfield, M.D.—*Healing the Child Within: Discovery and Recovery for Adult Children of Dysfunctional Families*

Marianne Williamson
- *A Return to Love*
- *Illuminate: A Return to Prayer*

Gary Zukav—*The Seat of the Soul*

In Gratitude

My life has been supported in so many ways. They say when the student is ready the teacher appears. This is really my story, teachers appearing to guide and show me the way all along sometimes veiled, sometimes recognizable. Starting with the elementary school teacher who let me write my own plays and perform them with stick figures for the class and another who first planted the idea that I had the potential to be somebody. Out of these seeds, hope, desire, and the drive to succeed were born. My early teachers and the ones to come were my salvation.

To my mother and the matriarchal lineage of my family who taught me discipline and hard work are the cornerstone of independence and rewards in themselves. To my Irish family who brought me full circle to home. To my loves past and present who teach me that compassion, unconditional love and understanding come in many forms. To the healers in all of their manifestations as energy workers, psychotherapists, authors, ministers and visionaries who healed my physical and emotional bodies so my spiritual form could take shape and emerge. To all the Soulfire Women, my mentors, my sisters in spirit, my friends, who have paved and opened the way for my walk, on whose foundation I stand daily. And lastly and most importantly to my daughter who is my greatest teacher of all… I AM in gratitude.

About Dyanne

As a writer, speaker, coach and psychotherapist, Dyanne connects you to the deepest, wisest part of yourself, your own authentic, true nature. She guides you in emotional self-healing at a transformational level to create lasting change. Through these experiences and through her personal healing journey, Dyanne discovered women have their own distinct pathway to healing and tending to the fire in their Soul, the flame within waiting to be remembered, reclaimed and reignited.

Dyanne is a prolific blogger, chronicling midlife in her blogs *Confessions from the Other Side... of 50* and *Traveling My Way – Midlife Misadventures with Dyanne Kelley,* observing life lessons with her dog in *Penelope and Me,* and teaching women how to step into their power in her blog *Soulfire Woman.*

Dyanne is a certified Journal to the Self instructor, Integrative Yoga Therapy teacher, Modern Day Wisdom Elder and Reconnective Healing Practitioner.

From Dyanne: Visit me at soulfirewoman.com for Soulfire Woman tools you can use in your own healing journey along with coaching, mentoring, and entertaining and informative blog posts and newsletters. I would love to meet you there and join you on your journey.

www.ingramcontent.com/pod-product-compliance
Lightning Source LLC
Chambersburg PA
CBHW060453080526
44584CB00015B/1425